MICHIGAN RULES OF PROFESS~~IONAL CONDUCT~~
2017 Edition

Updated through January 1, 2017

Michigan Legal Publishing Ltd.
QUICK DESK REFERENCE SERIES™

Academic and bulk discounts available at
www.michlp.com

WE WELCOME YOUR FEEDBACK: info@michlp.com

ISBN-13: 978-1-64002-003-0
ISBN-10: 1-64002-003-9

CONTENTS

MICHIGAN RULES OF PROFESSIONAL CONDUCT

Rule 1.0 Scope and Applicability

Rule: 1.0 Scope and Applicability of Rules and Commentary

(a) These are the Michigan Rules of Professional Conduct. The form of citation for this rule is MRPC 1.0.

(b) Failure to comply with an obligation or prohibition imposed by a rule is a basis for invoking the disciplinary process. The rules do not, however, give rise to a cause of action for enforcement of a rule or for damages caused by failure to comply with an obligation or prohibition imposed by a rule. In a civil or criminal action, the admissibility of the Rules of Professional Conduct is governed by the Michigan Rules of Evidence and other provisions of law.

(c) The text of each rule is authoritative. The comment that accompanies each rule does not expand or limit the scope of the obligations, prohibitions, and counsel found in the text of the rule.

Comment

The rules and comments were largely drawn from the American Bar Association's Model Rules of Professional Conduct. Prior to submission of those Model Rules to the Michigan Supreme Court, the State Bar of Michigan made minor changes in the rules and the comments to conform them to Michigan law and preferred practice. The Supreme Court then adopted the rules, with such substantive changes as appeared proper to the Court. Additional changes in the comments were then made by staff to conform the comments to the rules as adopted by the Supreme Court. The Supreme Court has authorized publication of the comments as an aid to the reader, but the rules alone comprise the Supreme Court's authoritative statement of a lawyer's ethical obligations.

PREAMBLE: A LAWYER'S RESPONSIBILITIES

This preamble is part of the comment to Rule 1.0, and provides a general introduction to the Rules of Professional Conduct.

A lawyer is a representative of clients, an officer of the legal system and a public citizen having special responsibility for the quality of justice.

As a representative of clients, a lawyer performs various functions. As advisor, a lawyer provides a client with an informed understanding of the client's legal rights and obligations and explains their practical implications. As advocate, a lawyer zealously asserts the client's position under the rules of the adversary system. As negotiator, a lawyer seeks a result advantageous to the

1

client but consistent with requirements of honest dealing with others. As intermediary between clients, a lawyer seeks to reconcile their divergent interests as an advisor and, to a limited extent, as a spokesperson for each client. A lawyer acts as evaluator by examining a client's legal affairs and reporting about them to the client or to others.

In all professional functions a lawyer should be competent, prompt and diligent. A lawyer should maintain communication with a client concerning the representation.

A lawyer should keep in confidence information relating to representation of a client except so far as disclosure is required or permitted by the Rules of Professional Conduct or other law.

A lawyer's conduct should conform to the requirements of the law, both in professional service to clients and in the lawyer's business and personal affairs. A lawyer should use the law's procedures only for legitimate purposes and not to harass or intimidate others. A lawyer should demonstrate respect for the legal system and for those who serve it, including judges, other lawyers and public officials. While it is a lawyer's duty, when necessary, to challenge the rectitude of official action, it is also a lawyer's duty to uphold legal process.

As a public citizen, a lawyer should seek improvement of the law, the administration of justice and the quality of service rendered by the legal profession. As a member of a learned profession, a lawyer should cultivate knowledge of the law beyond its use for clients, employ that knowledge in reform of the law and work to strengthen legal education. A lawyer should be mindful of deficiencies in the administration of justice and of the fact that the poor, and sometimes persons who are not poor, cannot afford adequate legal assistance, and should therefore devote professional time and civic influence in their behalf. A lawyer should aid the legal profession in pursuing these objectives and should help the bar regulate itself in the public interest.

Many of a lawyer's professional responsibilities are prescribed in the Rules of Professional Conduct, as well as substantive and procedural law. However, a lawyer is also guided by personal conscience and the approbation of professional peers. A lawyer should strive to attain the highest level of skill, to improve the law and the legal profession and to exemplify the legal profession's ideals of public service.

A lawyer's responsibilities as a representative of clients, an officer of the legal system, and a public citizen are usually harmonious. Thus, when an opposing party is well represented, a lawyer can be a zealous advocate on behalf of a client and at the same time assume that justice is being done. So also, a lawyer can be sure that preserving client confidences ordinarily serves the public interest because people are more likely to seek legal advice, and thereby heed their legal obligations, when they know their communications will be private.

In the nature of law practice, however, conflicting responsibilities are encountered. Virtually all difficult ethical problems arise from conflict between a lawyer's responsibilities to clients, to the legal system, and to the lawyer's own interest in remaining an upright person while earning a satisfactory living. The Rules of Professional Conduct prescribe terms for resolving such conflicts. Within the framework of these rules many difficult issues of professional discretion can arise. Such issues must be resolved through the exercise of sensitive professional and moral judgment guided by the basic principles underlying the rules.

The legal profession is largely self-governing. Although other professions also have been granted powers of self-government, the legal profession is unique in this respect because of the close relationship between the profession and the processes of government and law enforcement. This connection is manifested in the fact that ultimate authority over the legal profession is vested largely in the courts.

To the extent that lawyers meet the obligations of their professional calling, the occasion for government regulation is obviated. Self-regulation also helps maintain the legal profession's independence from government domination. An independent legal profession is an important force in preserving government under law, for abuse of legal authority is more readily challenged by a profession whose members are not dependent on government for the right to practice.

The legal profession's relative autonomy carries with it special responsibilities of self-government. The profession has a responsibility to assure that its regulations are conceived in the public interest and not in furtherance of parochial or self-interested concerns of the bar. Every lawyer is responsible for observance of the Rules of Professional Conduct. A lawyer should also aid in securing their observance by other lawyers. Neglect of these responsibilities compromises the independence of the profession and the public interest which it serves.

Lawyers play a vital role in the preservation of society. The fulfillment of this role requires an understanding by lawyers of their relationship to our legal system. The Rules of Professional Conduct, when properly applied, serve to define that relationship.

SCOPE

The Rules of Professional Conduct are rules of reason. They should be interpreted with reference to the purposes of legal representation and of the law itself. Some of the rules are imperatives, cast in the terms "shall" or "shall not." These define proper conduct for purposes of professional discipline. Others, generally cast in the term "may," are permissive and define areas under the rules in which the lawyer has professional discretion. No disciplinary action should be taken when the lawyer acts or chooses not to act within the bounds of such discretion. Other rules define the nature of relationships between the lawyer and others. The rules are thus partly obligatory and disciplinary and partly constitutive and descriptive in that they define a lawyer's professional role. Many of the comments use the term "should." Comments do not add obligations to the rules, but provide guidance for practicing in compliance with the rules.

The rules presuppose a larger legal context shaping the lawyer's role. That context includes court rules and statutes relating to matters of licensure, laws defining specific obligations of lawyers, and substantive and procedural law in general. Compliance with the rules, as with all law in an open society, depends primarily upon understanding and voluntary compliance, secondarily upon reinforcement by peer and public opinion, and finally, when necessary, upon enforcement through disciplinary proceedings. The rules do not, however, exhaust the moral and ethical considerations that should inform a lawyer, for no worthwhile human activity can be completely defined by legal rules. The rules simply provide a framework for the ethical practice of law.

Furthermore, for purposes of determining the lawyer's authority and responsibility, principles of substantive law external to these rules determine whether a client-lawyer relationship exists. Most of the duties flowing from the client-lawyer relationship attach only after the client has requested the lawyer to render legal services and the lawyer has agreed to do so. But there are some duties, such as that of confidentiality under Rule 1.6, that may attach when the lawyer agrees to consider whether a client-lawyer relationship shall be established. Whether a client-lawyer relationship exists for any specific purpose can depend on the circumstances and may be a question of fact.

Under various legal provisions, including constitutional, statutory and common-law, the responsibilities of government lawyers may include authority concerning legal matters that ordinarily reposes in the client in private client-lawyer relationships. For example, a lawyer for a government agency may have authority on behalf of the government to decide upon settlement or whether to appeal from an adverse judgment. Such authority in various respects is generally vested in the attorney general and the prosecuting attorney in state government, and their federal counterparts, and the same may be true of other government law officers. Also, lawyers under the supervision of these officers may be authorized to represent several government agencies in intragovernmental legal controversies in circumstances where a private lawyer could not represent multiple private clients. They also may have authority to represent the "public interest" in circumstances where a private lawyer would not be authorized to do so. These rules do not abrogate any such authority.

As indicated earlier in this comment, a failure to comply with an obligation or prohibition imposed by a rule is a basis for invoking the disciplinary process. The rules presuppose that disciplinary assessment of a lawyer's conduct will be made on the basis of the facts and circumstances as they existed at the time of the conduct in question and in recognition of the fact that a lawyer often has to act upon uncertain or incomplete evidence of the situation. Moreover, the rules presuppose that whether or not discipline should be imposed for a violation, and the severity of a sanction, depend on all the circumstances, such as the

4

willfulness and seriousness of the violation, extenuating factors and whether there have been previous violations.

As also indicated earlier in this comment, a violation of a rule does not give rise to a cause of action, nor does it create any presumption that a legal duty has been breached. The rules are designed to provide guidance to lawyers and to provide a structure for regulating conduct through disciplinary agencies. They are not designed to be a basis for civil liability. Furthermore, the purposes of the rules can be subverted when they are invoked by opposing parties as procedural weapons. The fact that a rule is a just basis for a lawyer's self-assessment, or for sanctioning a lawyer under the administration of a disciplinary authority, does not imply that an antagonist in a collateral proceeding or transaction has standing to seek enforcement of the rule. Accordingly, nothing in the rules should be deemed to augment any substantive legal duty of lawyers or the extradisciplinary consequences of violating such a duty.

Moreover, these rules are not intended to govern or affect judicial application of either the client-lawyer or work-product privilege. Those privileges were developed to promote compliance with law and fairness in litigation. In reliance on the client-lawyer privilege, clients are entitled to expect that communications within the scope of the privilege will be protected against compelled disclosure. The client-lawyer privilege is that of the client and not of the lawyer. The fact that in exceptional situations the lawyer under the rules has a limited discretion to disclose a client confidence does not vitiate the proposition that, as a general matter, the client has a reasonable expectation that information relating to the client will not be voluntarily disclosed and that disclosure of such information may be judicially compelled only in accordance with recognized exceptions to the client-lawyer and work-product privileges.

The lawyer's exercise of discretion not to disclose information under Rule 1.6 should not be subject to reexamination. Permitting such reexamination would be incompatible with the general policy of promoting compliance with law through assurances that communications will be protected against disclosure. The comment accompanying each rule explains and illustrates the meaning and purpose of the rule. The Preamble and this note on scope provide general orientation. The comments are intended as guides to interpretation, but the text of each rule is authoritative.

TERMINOLOGY

"Belief" or "believes" denotes that the person involved actually supposed the fact in question to be true. A person's belief may be inferred from circumstances.

"Consult" or "consultation" denotes communication of information reasonably sufficient to permit the client to appreciate the significance of the matter in question.

"Firm" or "law firm" denotes a lawyer or lawyers in a private firm, lawyers employed in the legal department of a corporation or other organization, and lawyers employed in a legal services organization. See comment, Rule 1.10.

"Fraud" or "fraudulent" denotes conduct having a purpose to deceive and not merely negligent misrepresentation or failure to apprise another of relevant information.

"Knowingly," "known," or "knows" denotes actual knowledge of the fact in question. A person's knowledge may be inferred from circumstances.

"Partner" denotes a member of a partnership and a shareholder in a law firm organized as a professional corporation.

"Reasonable" or "reasonably," when used in relation to conduct by a lawyer, denotes the conduct of a reasonably prudent and competent lawyer.

"Reasonable belief" or "reasonably believes," when used in reference to a lawyer, denotes that the lawyer believes the matter in question and that the circumstances are such that the belief is reasonable.

"Reasonably should know," when used in reference to a lawyer, denotes that a lawyer of reasonable prudence and competence would ascertain the matter in question.

"Substantial," when used in reference to degree or extent, denotes a material matter of clear and weighty importance.

Rules 1.1 - 1.17 Client-Lawyer Relationship

Rule: 1.1 Competence

A lawyer shall provide competent representation to a client. A lawyer shall not:
  (a) handle a legal matter which the lawyer knows or should know that the lawyer is not competent to handle, without associating with a lawyer who is competent to handle it;
  (b) handle a legal matter without preparation adequate in the circumstances; or
  (c) neglect a legal matter entrusted to the lawyer.

Comment

LEGAL KNOWLEDGE AND SKILL
    In determining whether a lawyer is able to provide competent representation in a particular matter, relevant factors include the relative

6

complexity and specialized nature of the matter, the lawyer's general experience, the lawyer's training and experience in the field in question, the preparation and study the lawyer is able to give the matter, and whether it is feasible to refer the matter to, or associate or consult with, a lawyer of established competence in the field in question. In many instances, the required proficiency is that of a general practitioner. Expertise in a particular field of law may be required in some circumstances.

A lawyer need not necessarily have special training or prior experience to handle legal problems of a type with which the lawyer is unfamiliar. A newly admitted lawyer can be as competent as a practitioner with long experience. Some important legal skills, such as the analysis of precedent, the evaluation of evidence and legal drafting, are required in all legal problems. Perhaps the most fundamental legal skill consists of determining what kind of legal problems a situation may involve, a skill that necessarily transcends any particular specialized knowledge. A lawyer can provide adequate representation in a wholly novel field through necessary study. Competent representation can also be provided through the association of a lawyer of established competence in the field in question.

In an emergency, a lawyer may give advice or assistance in a matter in which the lawyer does not have the skill ordinarily required where referral to or consultation or association with another lawyer would be impractical. Even in an emergency, however, assistance should be limited to that reasonably necessary in the circumstances, for ill-considered action under emergency conditions can jeopardize the client's interest.

A lawyer may offer representation where the requisite level of competence can be achieved by reasonable preparation. This applies as well to a lawyer who is appointed as counsel for an unrepresented person. See also Rule 6.2.

THOROUGHNESS AND PREPARATION
Competent handling of a particular matter includes inquiry into and analysis of the factual and legal elements of the problem, and use of methods and procedures meeting the standards of competent practitioners. It also includes adequate preparation. The required attention and preparation are determined in part by what is at stake; major litigation and complex transactions ordinarily require more elaborate treatment than matters of lesser consequence.

MAINTAINING COMPETENCE
To maintain the requisite knowledge and skill, a lawyer should engage in continuing study and education. If a system of peer review has been established, the lawyer should consider making use of it in appropriate circumstances.

Rule: 1.2 Scope of Representation

(a) A lawyer shall seek the lawful objectives of a client through reasonably available means permitted by law and these rules. A lawyer does not violate this rule by acceding to reasonable requests of opposing counsel that do not prejudice the rights of the client, by being punctual in fulfilling all professional commitments, or by avoiding offensive tactics. A lawyer shall abide by a client's decision whether to accept an offer of settlement or mediation evaluation of a matter. In a criminal case, the lawyer shall abide by the client's decision, after consultation with the lawyer, with respect to a plea to be entered, whether to waive jury trial, and whether the client will testify. In representing a client, a lawyer may, where permissible, exercise professional judgment to waive or fail to assert a right or position of the client.

(b) A lawyer may limit the objectives of the representation if the client consents after consultation.

(c) A lawyer shall not counsel a client to engage, or assist a client, in conduct that the lawyer knows is illegal or fraudulent, but a lawyer may discuss the legal consequences of any proposed course of conduct with a client and may counsel or assist a client to make a good-faith effort to determine the validity, scope, meaning, or application of the law.

(d) When a lawyer knows that a client expects assistance not permitted by the Rules of Professional Conduct or other law, the lawyer shall consult with the client regarding the relevant limitations on the lawyer's conduct.

Comment

SCOPE OF REPRESENTATION

Both the lawyer and the client have authority and responsibility in the objectives and means of representation. The client has ultimate authority to determine the purposes to be served by legal representation, within the limits imposed by law and the lawyer's professional obligations. Within those limits, a client also has a right to consult with the lawyer about the means to be used in pursuing those objectives. At the same time, a lawyer is not required to pursue objectives or employ means simply because a client may wish that the lawyer do so. A clear distinction between objectives and means sometimes cannot be drawn, and in many cases the client-lawyer relationship partakes of a joint undertaking. In questions of means, the lawyer should assume responsibility for technical and legal tactical issues, but should defer to the client regarding such questions as the expense to be incurred and concern for third persons who might be adversely affected.

In a case in which the client appears to be suffering mental disability, the lawyer's duty to abide by the client's decisions is to be guided by reference to Rule 1.14.

INDEPENDENCE FROM CLIENT'S VIEWS OR ACTIVITIES

Legal representation should not be denied to people who are unable to afford legal services or whose cause is controversial or the subject of popular disapproval. By the same token, representation of a client, including representation by appointment, does not constitute an endorsement of the client's political, economic, social, or moral views or activities.

SERVICES LIMITED IN OBJECTIVES OR MEANS

The objectives or scope of services provided by a lawyer may be limited by agreement with the client or by the terms under which the lawyer's services are made available to the client. For example, a retainer may be for a specifically defined purpose. Representation provided through a legal-aid agency may be subject to limitations on the types of cases the agency handles. When a lawyer has been retained by an insurer to represent an insured, the representation may be limited to matters related to the insurance coverage. The terms upon which representation is undertaken may exclude specific objectives or means. Such limitations may exclude objectives or means that the lawyer regards as repugnant or imprudent.

An agreement concerning the scope of representation must accord with the Rules of Professional Conduct and other law. Thus, the client may not be asked to agree to representation so limited in scope as to violate Rule 1.1, or to surrender the right to terminate the lawyer's services or the right to settle litigation that the lawyer might wish to continue.

ILLEGAL, FRAUDULENT, AND PROHIBITED TRANSACTIONS

A lawyer is required to give an honest opinion about the actual consequences that appear likely to result from a client's conduct. The fact that a client uses advice in a course of action that is illegal or fraudulent does not, of itself, make a lawyer a party to the course of action. However, a lawyer may not knowingly assist a client in illegal or fraudulent conduct. There is a critical distinction between presenting an analysis of legal aspects of questionable conduct and recommending the means by which an illegal act or fraud might be committed with impunity.

When the client's course of action has already begun and is continuing, the lawyer's responsibility is especially delicate. The lawyer is not permitted to reveal the client's wrongdoing, except where permitted by Rule 1.6. However, the lawyer is required to avoid furthering the purpose, for example, by suggesting how it might be concealed. A lawyer may not continue assisting a client in conduct that the lawyer originally supposes is legally proper but then discovers is illegal or fraudulent. Withdrawal from the representation, therefore, may be required.

Where the client is a fiduciary, the lawyer may be charged with special obligations in dealings with a beneficiary.

Paragraph (c) applies whether or not the defrauded party is a party to the transaction. Hence, a lawyer should not participate in a sham transaction; for example, a transaction to effectuate criminal or fraudulent escape of tax liability. Paragraph (c) does not preclude undertaking a criminal defense incident to a general retainer for legal services to a lawful enterprise. The last clause of paragraph (c) recognizes that determining the validity or interpretation of a statute or regulation may require a course of action involving disobedience of the statute or regulation or of the interpretation placed upon it by governmental authorities.

Rule: 1.3 Diligence

A lawyer shall act with reasonable diligence and promptness in representing a client.

Comment

A lawyer should pursue a matter on behalf of a client despite opposition, obstruction or personal inconvenience to the lawyer, and may take whatever lawful and ethical measures are required to vindicate a client's cause or endeavor. A lawyer should act with commitment and dedication to the interests of the client and with zeal in advocacy upon the client's behalf. However, a lawyer is not bound to press for every advantage that might be realized for a client. A lawyer has professional discretion in determining the means by which a matter should be pursued. See Rule 1.2. A lawyer's workload should be controlled so that each matter can be handled adequately.

Perhaps no professional shortcoming is more widely resented than procrastination. A client's interests often can be adversely affected by the passage of time or the change of conditions; in extreme instances, as when a lawyer overlooks a statute of limitations, the client's legal position may be destroyed. Even when the client's interests are not affected in substance, however, unreasonable delay can cause a client needless anxiety and undermine confidence in the lawyer's trustworthiness.

Unless the relationship is terminated as provided in Rule 1.16, a lawyer should carry through to conclusion all matters undertaken for a client. If a lawyer's employment is limited to a specific matter, the relationship terminates when the matter has been resolved. If a lawyer has served a client over a substantial period in a variety of matters, the client sometimes may assume that the lawyer will continue to serve on a continuing basis unless the lawyer gives notice of withdrawal. Doubt about whether a client-lawyer relationship still exists should be clarified by the lawyer, preferably in writing, so that the client will not mistakenly suppose the lawyer is looking after the client's affairs when the lawyer has ceased to do so. For example, if a lawyer has handled a judicial or administrative proceeding that produced a result adverse to the client but has not been specifically instructed concerning pursuit of an appeal, the lawyer should advise the client of the possibility of appeal before relinquishing responsibility for the matter.

Rule: 1.4 Communication

(a) A lawyer shall keep a client reasonably informed about the status of a matter and comply promptly with reasonable requests for information. A lawyer shall notify the client promptly of all settlement offers, mediation evaluations, and proposed plea bargains.
(b) A lawyer shall explain a matter to the extent reasonably necessary to permit the client to make informed decisions regarding the representation.

Comment

The client should have sufficient information to participate intelligently in decisions concerning the objectives of the representation and the means by which they are to be pursued to the extent the client is willing and able to do so. For example, a lawyer negotiating on behalf of a client should provide the client with facts relevant to the matter, inform the client of communications from another party, and take other reasonable steps that permit the client to make a decision regarding an offer from another party. A lawyer who receives an offer of settlement or a mediation evaluation in a civil controversy, or a proffered plea bargain in a criminal case, must promptly inform the client of its substance. See Rule 1.2(a). Even when a client delegates authority to the lawyer, the client should be kept advised of the status of the matter.

Adequacy of communication depends in part on the kind of advice or assistance involved. For example, in negotiations where there is time to explain a proposal, the lawyer should review all important provisions with the client before proceeding to an agreement. In litigation, a lawyer should explain the general strategy and prospects of success and ordinarily should consult the client on tactics that might injure or coerce others. On the other hand, a lawyer ordinarily cannot be expected to describe trial or negotiation strategy in detail. The guiding principle is that the lawyer should fulfill reasonable client expectations for information consistent with the duty to act in the client's best interests and consistent with the client's overall requirements as to the character of representation.

Ordinarily, the information to be provided is that appropriate for a client who is a comprehending and responsible adult. However, fully informing the client according to this standard may be impracticable, for example, where the client is a child or suffers from mental disability. See Rule 1.14. When the client is an organization or group, it is often impossible or inappropriate to inform every one of its members about its legal affairs; ordinarily, the lawyer should address communications to the appropriate officials of the organization. See Rule 1.13. Where many routine matters are involved, a system of limited or occasional reporting may be arranged with the client. Practical exigency may also require a lawyer to act for a client without prior consultation.

WITHHOLDING INFORMATION

In some circumstances, a lawyer may be justified in delaying transmission of information when the client would be likely to react imprudently to an immediate communication. Thus, a lawyer might withhold a psychiatric diagnosis of a client when the examining psychiatrist indicates that disclosure would harm the client. A lawyer may not withhold information to serve the lawyer's own interest or convenience. Rules or court orders governing litigation may provide that information supplied to a lawyer may not be disclosed to the client. Rule 3.4(c) directs compliance with such rules or orders.

Rule: 1.5 Fees

(a) A lawyer shall not enter into an agreement for, charge, or collect an illegal or clearly excessive fee. A fee is clearly excessive when, after a review of the facts, a lawyer of ordinary prudence would be left with a definite and firm conviction that the fee is in excess of a reasonable fee. The factors to be considered in determining the reasonableness of a fee include the following:
   (1) the time and labor required, the novelty and difficulty of the questions involved, and the skill requisite to perform the legal service properly;
   (2) the likelihood, if apparent to the client, that the acceptance of the particular employment will preclude other employment by the lawyer;
   (3) the fee customarily charged in the locality for similar legal services;
   (4) the amount involved and the results obtained;
   (5) the time limitations imposed by the client or by the circumstances;
   (6) the nature and length of the professional relationship with the client;
   (7) the experience, reputation, and ability of the lawyer or lawyers performing the services; and
   (8) whether the fee is fixed or contingent.

(b) When the lawyer has not regularly represented the client, the basis or rate of the fee shall be communicated to the client, preferably in writing, before or within a reasonable time after commencing the representation.

(c) A fee may be contingent on the outcome of the matter for which the service is rendered, except in a matter in which a contingent fee is prohibited by paragraph (d) or by other law. A contingent-fee agreement shall be in writing and shall state the method by which the fee is to be determined. Upon conclusion of a contingent-fee matter, the lawyer shall provide the client with a written statement of the outcome of the matter and, if there is a recovery, show the remittance to the client and the method of its determination. See also MCR 8.121 for additional requirements applicable to some contingent-fee agreements.

(d) A lawyer shall not enter into an arrangement for, charge, or collect a contingent fee in a domestic relations matter or in a criminal matter.

(e) A division of a fee between lawyers who are not in the same firm may be made only if:
   (1) the client is advised of and does not object to the participation of all the lawyers involved; and
   (2) the total fee is reasonable.

Comment

BASIS OR RATE OF FEE

When the lawyer has regularly represented a client, they ordinarily will have evolved an understanding concerning the basis or rate of the fee. In a new client-lawyer relationship, however, an understanding as to the fee should be promptly established. It is not necessary to recite all the factors that underlie the basis of the fee, but only those that are directly involved in its computation. It is sufficient, for example, to state that the basic rate is an hourly charge or a fixed amount or an estimated amount, or to identify the factors that may be taken into account in finally fixing the fee. When developments occur during the representation that render an earlier estimate substantially inaccurate, a revised estimate should be provided to the client. A written statement concerning the fee reduces the possibility of misunderstanding. Furnishing the client with a simple memorandum or a copy of the lawyer's customary fee schedule is sufficient if the basis or rate of the fee is set forth.

TERMS OF PAYMENT

A lawyer may require advance payment of a fee, but is obliged to return any unearned portion. See Rule 1.16(d). A lawyer may accept property in payment for services, such as an ownership interest in an enterprise, providing this does not involve acquisition of a proprietary interest in the cause of action or subject matter of the litigation contrary to Rule 1.8(j). However, a fee paid in property instead of money may be subject to special scrutiny because it involves questions concerning both the value of the services and the lawyer's special knowledge of the value of the property.

An agreement may not be made whose terms might induce the lawyer improperly to curtail services for the client or perform them in a way contrary to the client's interest. For example, a lawyer should not enter into an agreement whereby services are to be provided only up to a stated amount when it is foreseeable that more extensive services probably will be required, unless the situation is adequately explained to the client. Otherwise, the client might have to bargain for further assistance in the midst of a proceeding or transaction. However, it is proper to define the extent of services in light of the client's ability to pay. A lawyer should not exploit a fee arrangement based primarily on hourly charges by using wasteful procedures. When there is doubt whether a contingent fee is consistent with the client's best interest, the lawyer should offer the client alternative bases for the fee and explain their implications. Applicable law may impose limitations on contingent fees, such as a ceiling on the percentage. See MCR 8.121.

DIVISION OF FEE
A division of fee is a single billing to a client covering the fee of two or more lawyers who are not in the same firm. A division of fee facilitates association of more than one lawyer in a matter in which neither alone could serve the client as well, and most often is used when the fee is contingent and the division is between a referring lawyer and a trial specialist. Paragraph (e) permits the lawyers to divide a fee on agreement between the participating lawyers if the client is advised and does not object. It does not require disclosure to the client of the share that each lawyer is to receive.

DISPUTES OVER FEES
If a procedure has been established for resolution of fee disputes, such as an arbitration or mediation procedure established by the bar, the lawyer should conscientiously consider submitting to it. Law may prescribe a procedure for determining a lawyer's fee, for example, in representation of an executor or administrator, of a class, or of a person entitled to a reasonable fee as part of the measure of damages. The lawyer entitled to such a fee and a lawyer representing another party concerned with the fee should comply with the prescribed procedure.

Rule: 1.6 Confidentiality of Information

(a) "Confidence" refers to information protected by the client-lawyer privilege under applicable law, and "secret" refers to other information gained in the professional relationship that the client has requested be held inviolate or the disclosure of which would be embarrassing or would be likely to be detrimental to the client.

(b) Except when permitted under paragraph (c), a lawyer shall not knowingly:
    (1) reveal a confidence or secret of a client;
    (2) use a confidence or secret of a client to the disadvantage of the client; or
    (3) use a confidence or secret of a client for the advantage of the lawyer or of a third person, unless the client consents after full disclosure.

(c) A lawyer may reveal:
    (1) confidences or secrets with the consent of the client or clients affected, but only after full disclosure to them;
    (2) confidences or secrets when permitted or required by these rules, or when required by law or by court order;
    (3) confidences and secrets to the extent reasonably necessary to rectify the consequences of a client's illegal or fraudulent act in the furtherance of which the lawyer's services have been used;
    (4) the intention of a client to commit a crime and the information necessary to prevent the crime; and
    (5) confidences or secrets necessary to establish or collect a fee, or to defend the lawyer or the lawyer's employees or associates against an accusation of wrongful conduct.

(d) A lawyer shall exercise reasonable care to prevent employees, associates, and others whose services are utilized by the lawyer from disclosing or using confidences or secrets of a client, except that a lawyer may reveal the information allowed by paragraph (c) through an employee.

Comment

The lawyer is part of a judicial system charged with upholding the law. One of the lawyer's functions is to advise clients so that they avoid any violation of the law in the proper exercise of their rights.

The observance of the ethical obligation of a lawyer to hold inviolate confidential information of the client not only facilitates the full development of facts essential to proper representation of the client, but also encourages people to seek early legal assistance.

Almost without exception, clients come to lawyers in order to determine what their rights are and what is, in the maze of laws and regulations, deemed to be legal and correct. The common law recognizes that the client's confidences must be protected from disclosure. Upon the basis of experience, lawyers know that almost all clients follow the advice given and that the law is upheld.

A fundamental principle in the client-lawyer relationship is that the lawyer maintain confidentiality of information relating to the representation. The client is thereby encouraged to communicate fully and frankly with the lawyer even as to embarrassing or legally damaging subject matter.

The principle of confidentiality is given effect in two related bodies of law, the client-lawyer privilege (which includes the work-product doctrine) in the law of evidence and the rule of confidentiality established in professional ethics. The client-lawyer privilege applies in judicial and other proceedings in which a lawyer may be called as a witness or otherwise required to produce evidence concerning a client. The rule of client-lawyer confidentiality applies in situations other than those where evidence is sought from the lawyer through compulsion of law. The confidentiality rule applies to confidences and secrets as defined in the rule. A lawyer may not disclose such information except as authorized or required by the Rules of Professional Conduct or other law. See also Scope, ante, p M 1-18.

The requirement of maintaining confidentiality of information relating to representation applies to government lawyers who may disagree with the policy goals that their representation is designed to advance.

AUTHORIZED DISCLOSURE

A lawyer is impliedly authorized to make disclosures about a client when appropriate in carrying out the representation, except to the extent that the client's instructions or special circumstances limit that authority. In litigation, for example, a lawyer may disclose information by admitting a fact that cannot properly be disputed, or, in negotiation, by making a disclosure that facilitates a satisfactory conclusion.

Lawyers in a firm may, in the course of the firm's practice, disclose to each other information relating to a client of the firm, unless the client has instructed that particular information be confined to specified lawyers, or unless the disclosure would breach a screen erected within the firm in accordance with Rules 1.10(b), 1.11(a), or 1.12(c).

DISCLOSURE ADVERSE TO CLIENT

The confidentiality rule is subject to limited exceptions. In becoming privy to information about a client, a lawyer may foresee that the client intends to commit a crime. To the extent a lawyer is prohibited from making disclosure, the interests of the potential victim are sacrificed in favor of preserving the client's confidences even though the client's purpose is wrongful. To the extent a lawyer is required or permitted to disclose a client's purposes, the client may be inhibited from revealing facts which would enable the lawyer to counsel against a wrongful course of action. A rule governing disclosure of threatened harm thus involves balancing the interests of one group of potential victims against those of another. On the assumption that lawyers generally fulfill their duty to advise against the commission of deliberately wrongful acts, the public is better protected if full and open communication by the client is encouraged than if it is inhibited.

Generally speaking, information relating to the representation must be kept confidential as stated in paragraph (b). However, when the client is or will be engaged in criminal conduct or the integrity of the lawyer's own conduct is involved, the principle of confidentiality may appropriately yield, depending on the lawyer's knowledge about and relationship to the conduct in question, and the seriousness of that conduct. Several situations must be distinguished.

First, the lawyer may not counsel or assist a client in conduct that is illegal or fraudulent. See Rule 1.2(c). Similarly, a lawyer has a duty under Rule 3.3(a)(4) not to use false evidence. This duty is essentially a special instance of the duty prescribed in Rule 1.2(c) to avoid assisting a client in illegal or fraudulent conduct. The same is true of compliance with Rule 4.1 concerning truthfulness of a lawyer's own representations.

Second, the lawyer may have been innocently involved in past conduct by the client that was criminal or fraudulent. In such a situation the lawyer has not violated Rule 1.2(c), because to "counsel or assist" criminal or fraudulent conduct requires knowing that the conduct is of that character. Even if the involvement was innocent, however, the fact remains that the lawyer's professional services were made the instrument of the client's crime or fraud. The lawyer, therefore, has a legitimate interest in being able to rectify the consequences of such conduct, and has the professional right, although not a professional duty, to rectify the situation. Exercising that right may require revealing information relating to the representation. Paragraph (c)(3) gives the lawyer professional discretion to reveal such information to the extent necessary to accomplish rectification. However, the constitutional rights of defendants in criminal cases may limit the extent to which counsel for a defendant may correct a misrepresentation that is based on information provided by the client. See comment to Rule 3.3.

Third, the lawyer may learn that a client intends prospective conduct that is criminal. Inaction by the lawyer is not a violation of Rule 1.2(c), except in the limited circumstances where failure to act constitutes assisting the client. See comment to Rule 1.2(c). However, the lawyer's knowledge of the client's purpose may enable the lawyer to prevent commission of the prospective crime. If the prospective crime is likely to result in substantial injury, the lawyer may feel a moral obligation to take preventive action. When the threatened injury is grave, such as homicide or serious bodily injury, a lawyer may have an obligation under tort or criminal law to take reasonable preventive measures. Whether the lawyer's concern is based on moral or legal considerations, the interest in preventing the harm may be more compelling than the interest in preserving confidentiality of information relating to the client. As stated in paragraph (c)(4), the lawyer has professional discretion to reveal information in order to prevent a client's criminal act.

It is arguable that the lawyer should have a professional obligation to make a disclosure in order to prevent homicide or serious bodily injury which the lawyer knows is intended by the client. However, it is very difficult for a lawyer to "know" when such a heinous purpose will actually be carried out, for the client may have a change of mind. To require disclosure when the client intends such an act, at the risk of professional discipline if the assessment of the client's purpose turns out to be wrong, would be to impose a penal risk that might interfere with the lawyer's resolution of an inherently difficult moral dilemma.

The lawyer's exercise of discretion requires consideration of such factors as magnitude, proximity, and likelihood of the contemplated wrong; the nature of the lawyer's relationship with the client and with those who might be injured by the client; the lawyer's own involvement in the transaction; and factors that may extenuate the conduct in question. Where practical, the lawyer should seek to persuade the client to take suitable action. In any case, a disclosure adverse to the client's interest should be no greater than the lawyer reasonably believes necessary to the purpose. A lawyer's decision not to make a disclosure permitted by paragraph (c) does not violate this rule.

Where the client is an organization, the lawyer may be in doubt whether contemplated conduct will actually be carried out by the organization. Where necessary to guide conduct in connection with this rule, the lawyer should make an inquiry within the organization as indicated in Rule 1.13(b).

Paragraph (c)(3) does not apply where a lawyer is employed after a crime or fraud has been committed to represent the client in matters ensuing therefrom.

WITHDRAWAL

If the lawyer's services will be used by the client in materially furthering a course of criminal or fraudulent conduct, the lawyer must withdraw, as stated in Rule 1.16(a)(1).

After withdrawal the lawyer is required to refrain from making disclosure of the client's confidences, except as otherwise provided in Rule 1.6. Neither this rule nor Rule 1.8(b) nor Rule 1.16(d) prevents the lawyer from giving notice of the fact of withdrawal, and the lawyer may also withdraw or disaffirm any opinion, document, affirmation, or the like.

DISPUTE CONCERNING LAWYER'S CONDUCT

Where a legal claim or disciplinary charge alleges complicity of the lawyer in a client's conduct or other misconduct of the lawyer involving representation of the client, the lawyer may respond to the extent the lawyer reasonably believes necessary to establish a defense. The same is true with respect to a claim involving the conduct or representation of a former client. The lawyer's right to respond arises when an assertion of complicity or other misconduct has been made. Paragraph (c)(5) does not require the lawyer to await the commencement of an action or proceeding that charges complicity or other misconduct, so that the defense may be established by responding directly to a third party who has made such an assertion. The right to defend, of course, applies where a proceeding has been commenced. Where practicable and not prejudicial to the lawyer's ability to establish the defense, the lawyer should advise the client of the third party's assertion and request that the client respond appropriately. In any event, disclosure should be no greater than the lawyer reasonably believes is necessary to vindicate innocence, the disclosure should be made in a manner which limits access to the information to the tribunal or other persons having a need to know it, and appropriate protective orders or other arrangements should be sought by the lawyer to the fullest extent practicable.

If the lawyer is charged with wrongdoing in which the client's conduct is implicated, the rule of confidentiality should not prevent the lawyer from defending against the charge. Such a charge can arise in a civil, criminal, or professional disciplinary proceeding, and can be based on a wrong allegedly committed by the lawyer against the client, or on a wrong alleged by a third person, for example, a person claiming to have been defrauded by the lawyer and client acting together.

A lawyer entitled to a fee is permitted by paragraph (c)(5) to prove the services rendered in an action to collect it. This aspect of the rule expresses the principle that the beneficiary of a fiduciary relationship may not exploit it to the detriment of the fiduciary. As stated above, the lawyer must make every effort practicable to avoid unnecessary disclosure of information relating to a representation, to limit disclosure to those having the need to know it, and to obtain protective orders or make other arrangements minimizing the risk of disclosure.

DISCLOSURES OTHERWISE REQUIRED OR AUTHORIZED

The scope of the client-lawyer privilege is a question of law. If a lawyer is called as a witness to give testimony concerning a client, absent waiver by the client, paragraph (b)(1) requires the lawyer to invoke the privilege when it is applicable. The lawyer must comply with the final orders of a court or other tribunal of competent jurisdiction requiring the lawyer to give information about the client.

The Rules of Professional Conduct in various circumstances permit or require a lawyer to disclose information relating to the representation. See Rules 2.2, 2.3, 3.3 and 4.1. In addition to these provisions, a lawyer may be obligated or permitted by other provisions of law to give information about a client. Whether another provision of law supersedes Rule 1.6 is a matter of interpretation beyond the scope of these rules, but a presumption should exist against such a supersession.

FORMER CLIENT

The duty of confidentiality continues after the client-lawyer relationship has terminated. See Rule 1.9.

Rule: 1.7 Conflict of Interest: General Rule

(a) A lawyer shall not represent a client if the representation of that client will be directly adverse to another client, unless:

    (1) the lawyer reasonably believes the representation will not adversely affect the relationship with the other client; and

    (2) each client consents after consultation.

(b) A lawyer shall not represent a client if the representation of that client may be materially limited by the lawyer's responsibilities to another client or to a third person, or by the lawyer's own interests, unless:

    (1) the lawyer reasonably believes the representation will not be adversely affected; and

    (2) the client consents after consultation. When representation of multiple clients in a single matter is undertaken, the consultation shall include explanation of the implications of the common representation and the advantages and risks involved.

Comment

LOYALTY TO A CLIENT

Loyalty is an essential element in the lawyer's relationship to a client. An impermissible conflict of interest may exist before representation is undertaken, in which event the representation should be declined. The lawyer should adopt reasonable procedures, appropriate for the size and type of firm and practice, to determine in both litigation and nonlitigation matters the parties and issues involved and to determine whether there are actual or potential conflicts of interest.

If such a conflict arises after representation has been undertaken, the lawyer should withdraw from the representation. See Rule 1.16. Where more than one client is involved and the lawyer withdraws because a conflict arises after representation, whether the lawyer may continue to represent any of the clients is determined by Rule 1.9. See also Rule 2.2(c). As to whether a client-lawyer relationship exists or, having once been established, is continuing, see comment to Rule 1.3 and Scope, ante, p M 1-18.

As a general proposition, loyalty to a client prohibits undertaking representation directly adverse to that client without that client's consent. Paragraph (a) expresses that general rule. Thus, a lawyer ordinarily may not act as advocate against a person the lawyer represents in some other matter, even if it is wholly unrelated. On the other hand, simultaneous representation in unrelated matters of clients whose interests are only generally adverse, such as competing economic enterprises, does not require consent of the respective clients. Paragraph (a) applies only when the representation of one client would be directly adverse to the other.

Loyalty to a client is also impaired when a lawyer cannot consider, recommend, or carry out an appropriate course of action for the client because of the lawyer's other responsibilities or interests. The conflict in effect forecloses alternatives that would otherwise be available to the client. Paragraph (b) addresses such situations. A possible conflict does not itself preclude the representation. The critical questions are the likelihood that a conflict will eventuate and, if it does, whether it will materially interfere with the lawyer's independent professional judgment in considering alternatives or foreclose courses of action that reasonably should be pursued on behalf of the client. Consideration should be given to whether the client wishes to accommodate the other interest involved.

CONSULTATION AND CONSENT

A client may consent to representation notwithstanding a conflict. However, as indicated in paragraph (a)(1) with respect to representation directly adverse to a client, and paragraph (b)(1) with respect to material limitations on representation of a client, when a disinterested lawyer would conclude that the client should not agree to the representation under the circumstances, the lawyer involved cannot properly ask for such agreement or provide representation on the basis of the client's consent. When more than one client is involved, the question of conflict must be resolved as to each client. Moreover, there may be circumstances where it is impossible to make the disclosure necessary to obtain consent. For example, when the lawyer represents different clients in related matters and one of the clients refuses to consent to the disclosure necessary to permit the other client to make an informed decision, the lawyer cannot properly ask the latter to consent.

LAWYER'S INTERESTS

The lawyer's own interests should not be permitted to have adverse effect on representation of a client. For example, a lawyer's need for income should not lead the lawyer to undertake matters that cannot be handled competently and at a reasonable fee. See Rules 1.1 and 1.5. If the probity of a lawyer's own conduct in a transaction is in serious question, it may be difficult or impossible for the lawyer to give a client detached advice. A lawyer may not allow related business interests to affect representation, for example, by referring clients to an enterprise in which the lawyer has an undisclosed interest.

CONFLICTS IN LITIGATION

Paragraph (a) prohibits representation of opposing parties in litigation. Simultaneous representation of parties whose interests in litigation may conflict, such as coplaintiffs or codefendants, is governed by paragraph (b). An impermissible conflict may exist by reason of substantial discrepancy in the parties' testimony, incompatibility in positions in relation to an opposing party, or the fact that there are substantially different possibilities of settlement of the claims or liabilities in question. Such conflicts can arise in criminal cases as well as civil. The potential for conflict of interest in representing multiple defendants in a criminal case is so grave that ordinarily a lawyer should decline to represent more than one codefendant. On the other hand, common representation of persons having similar interests is proper if the risk of adverse effect is minimal and the requirements of paragraph (b) are met. Compare Rule 2.2 involving intermediation between clients.

Ordinarily, a lawyer may not act as advocate against a client the lawyer represents in some other matter, even if the other matter is wholly unrelated. However, there are circumstances in which a lawyer may act as advocate against a client. For example, a lawyer representing an enterprise with diverse operations may accept employment as an advocate against the enterprise in an unrelated matter if doing so will not adversely affect the lawyer's relationship with the enterprise or conduct of the suit and if both clients consent upon consultation. By the same token, government lawyers in some circumstances may represent government employees in proceedings in which a government agency is the opposing party. The propriety of concurrent representation can depend on the nature of the litigation. For example, a suit charging fraud entails conflict to a degree not involved in a suit for a declaratory judgment concerning statutory interpretation.

INTEREST OF PERSON PAYING FOR A LAWYER'S SERVICE

A lawyer may be paid from a source other than the client if the client is informed of that fact and consents and the arrangement does not compromise the lawyer's duty of loyalty to the client. See Rule 1.8(f). For example, when an insurer and its insured have conflicting interests in a matter arising from a liability insurance agreement, and the insurer is required to provide special counsel for the insured, the arrangement should assure the special counsel's professional independence. So also, when a corporation and its directors or employees are involved in a controversy in which they have conflicting interests, the corporation may provide funds for separate legal representation of the directors or employees if the clients consent after consultation and the arrangement ensures the lawyer's professional independence.

OTHER CONFLICT SITUATIONS

Conflicts of interest in contexts other than litigation sometimes may be difficult to assess. Relevant factors in determining whether there is potential for adverse effect include the duration and intimacy of the lawyer's relationship with the client or clients involved, the functions being performed by the lawyer, the likelihood that actual conflict will arise, and the likely prejudice to the client from the conflict if it does arise. The question is often one of proximity and degree.

For example, a lawyer may not represent multiple parties in a negotiation whose interests are fundamentally antagonistic to each other, but common representation is permissible where the clients are generally aligned in interest even though there is some difference of interest among them.

Conflict questions may also arise in estate planning and estate administration. A lawyer may be called upon to prepare wills for several family members, such as husband and wife, and, depending upon the circumstances, a conflict of interest may arise. In estate administration the identity of the client may be a question of law. The lawyer should make clear the relationship to the parties involved.

A lawyer for a corporation or other organization who is also a member of its board of directors should determine whether the responsibilities of the two roles may conflict. The lawyer may be called on to advise the corporation in matters involving actions of the directors. Consideration should be given to the frequency with which such situations may arise, the potential intensity of the conflict, the effect of the lawyer's resignation from the board, and the possibility of the corporation's obtaining legal advice from another lawyer in such situations. If there is material risk that the dual role will compromise the lawyer's independence of professional judgment, the lawyer should not serve as a director.

CONFLICT CHARGED BY AN OPPOSING PARTY

Resolving questions of conflict of interest is primarily the responsibility of the lawyer undertaking the representation. In litigation, a court may raise the question when there is reason to infer that the lawyer has neglected the responsibility. In a criminal case, inquiry by the court is generally required when a lawyer represents multiple defendants. See MCR 6.101(C)(4). Where the conflict is such as clearly to call in question the fair or efficient administration of justice, opposing counsel may properly raise the question. Such an objection should be viewed with caution, however, for it can be misused as a technique of harassment. See Scope, ante, p M 1-18.

Rule: 1.8 Conflict of Interest: Prohibited Transactions

(a) A lawyer shall not enter into a business transaction with a client or knowingly acquire an ownership, possessory, security, or other pecuniary interest adverse to a client unless:

   (1) the transaction and terms on which the lawyer acquires the interest are fair and reasonable to the client and are fully disclosed and transmitted in writing to the client in a manner that can be reasonably understood by the client;

   (2) the client is given a reasonable opportunity to seek the advice of independent counsel in the transaction; and

   (3) the client consents in writing thereto.

(b) A lawyer shall not use information relating to representation of a client to the disadvantage of the client unless the client consents after consultation, except as permitted or required by Rule 1.6 or Rule 3.3.

(c) A lawyer shall not prepare an instrument giving the lawyer or a person related to the lawyer as parent, child, sibling, or spouse any substantial gift from a client, including a testamentary gift, except where the client is related to the donee.

(d) Prior to the conclusion of representation of a client, a lawyer shall not make or negotiate an agreement giving the lawyer literary or media rights to a portrayal or account based in substantial part on information relating to the representation.

(e) A lawyer shall not provide financial assistance to a client in connection with pending or contemplated litigation, except that

   (1) a lawyer may advance court costs and expenses of litigation, the repayment of which shall ultimately be the responsibility of the client; and

   (2) a lawyer representing an indigent client may pay court costs and expenses of litigation on behalf of the client.

(f) A lawyer shall not accept compensation for representing a client from one other than the client unless:

   (1) the client consents after consultation;

   (2) there is no interference with the lawyer's independence of professional judgment or with the client-lawyer relationship; and

   (3) information relating to representation of a client is protected as required by Rule 1.6.

(g) A lawyer who represents two or more clients shall not participate in making an aggregate settlement of the claims of or against the clients, or, in a criminal case, an aggregated agreement as to guilty or nolo contendere pleas, unless each client consents after consultation, including disclosure of the existence and nature of all the claims or pleas involved and of the participation of each person in the settlement.

(h) A lawyer shall not:
    (1) make an agreement prospectively limiting the lawyer's liability to a client for malpractice unless permitted by law and the client is independently represented in making the agreement; or
    (2) settle a claim for such liability with an unrepresented client or former client without first advising that person in writing that independent representation is appropriate in connection therewith.
(i) A lawyer related to another lawyer as parent, child, sibling, or spouse shall not represent a client in a representation directly adverse to a person whom the lawyer knows is represented by the other lawyer except upon consent by the client after consultation regarding the relationship.
(j) A lawyer shall not acquire a proprietary interest in the cause of action or subject matter of litigation the lawyer is conducting for a client, except that the lawyer may:
    (1) acquire a lien granted by law to secure the lawyer's fee or expenses; and
    (2) contract with a client for a reasonable contingent fee in a civil case, as permitted by Rule 1.5 and MCR 8.121.

Comment

TRANSACTIONS BETWEEN CLIENT AND LAWYER

As a general principle, all transactions between client and lawyer should be fair and reasonable to the client. In such transactions a review by independent counsel on behalf of the client is often advisable. Furthermore, a lawyer may not exploit information relating to the representation to the client's disadvantage. For example, a lawyer who has learned that the client is investing in specific real estate may not, without the client's consent, seek to acquire nearby property where doing so would adversely affect the client's plan for investment. Paragraph (a) does not, however, apply to standard commercial transactions between the lawyer and the client for products or services that the client generally markets to others, for example, banking or brokerage services, medical services, products manufactured or distributed by the client, and utilities' services. In such transactions, the lawyer has no advantage in dealing with the client, and the restrictions in paragraph (a) are unnecessary and impracticable.

A lawyer may accept a gift from a client if the transaction meets general standards of fairness. For example, a simple gift such as a present given at a holiday or as a token of appreciation is permitted. If effectuation of a substantial gift requires preparing a legal instrument such as a will or conveyance, however, the client should have the detached advice that another lawyer can provide. Paragraph (c) recognizes an exception where the client is a relative of the donee or the gift is not substantial.

LITERARY RIGHTS

An agreement by which a lawyer acquires literary or media rights concerning the conduct of the representation creates a conflict between the interests of the client and the personal interests of the lawyer. Measures suitable in the representation of the client may detract from the publication value of an account of the representation. Paragraph (d) does not prohibit a lawyer representing a client in a transaction concerning literary property from agreeing that the lawyer's fee shall consist of a share in ownership in the property, if the arrangement conforms to Rule 1.5 and paragraph (j).

PERSON PAYING FOR LAWYER'S SERVICES

Paragraph (f) requires disclosure of the fact that the lawyer's services are being paid for by a third party. Such an arrangement must also conform to the requirements of Rule 1.6 concerning confidentiality and Rule 1.7 concerning conflict of interest. Where the client is a class, consent may be obtained on behalf of the class by court-supervised procedure.

LIMITING LIABILITY

Paragraph (h) is not intended to apply to customary qualifications and limitations in legal opinions and memoranda.

FAMILY RELATIONSHIPS BETWEEN LAWYERS

Paragraph (i) applies to related lawyers who are in different firms. Related lawyers in the same firm are governed by Rules 1.7, 1.9, and 1.10. The disqualification stated in paragraph (i) is personal and is not imputed to members of firms with whom the lawyers are associated.

ACQUISITION OF INTEREST IN LITIGATION

Paragraph (j) states the traditional general rule that lawyers are prohibited from acquiring a proprietary interest in litigation. This general rule, which has its basis in common-law champerty and maintenance, is subject to specific exceptions developed in decisional law and continued in these rules, such as the exception for reasonable contingent fees set forth in Rule 1.5 and the exception for certain advances of the costs of litigation set forth in paragraph (e).

SEXUAL RELATIONS WITH CLIENTS

After careful study, the Supreme Court declined in 1998 to adopt a proposal to amend Rule 1.8 to limit sexual relationships between lawyers and clients. The Michigan Rules of Professional Conduct adequately prohibit representation that lacks competence or diligence, or that is shadowed by a conflict of interest. With regard to sexual behavior, the Michigan Court Rules provide that a lawyer may be disciplined for "conduct that is contrary to justice, ethics, honesty, or good morals." MCR 9.104(3). Further, the Legislature has enacted criminal penalties for certain types of sexual misconduct. In this regard, it should be emphasized that a lawyer bears a fiduciary responsibility toward the client. A lawyer who has a conflict of interest, whose actions interfere with effective representation, who takes advantage of a client's vulnerability, or whose behavior is immoral risks severe sanctions under the existing Michigan Court Rules and Michigan Rules of Professional Conduct.

Rule: 1.9 Conflict of Interest: Former Client

(a) A lawyer who has formerly represented a client in a matter shall not thereafter represent another person in the same or a substantially related matter in which that person's interests are materially adverse to the interests of the former client unless the former client consents after consultation.

(b) Unless the former client consents after consultation, a lawyer shall not knowingly represent a person in the same or a substantially related matter in which a firm with which the lawyer formerly was associated has previously represented a client
    (1) whose interests are materially adverse to that person, and
    (2) about whom the lawyer had acquired information protected by Rules 1.6 and 1.9(c) that is material to the matter.

(c) A lawyer who has formerly represented a client in a matter or whose present or former firm has formerly represented a client in a matter shall not thereafter:
    (1) use information relating to the representation to the disadvantage of the former client except as Rule 1.6 or Rule 3.3 would permit or require with respect to a client, or when the information has become generally known; or
    (2) reveal information relating to the representation except as Rule 1.6 or Rule 3.3 would permit or require with respect to a client.

Comment

After termination of a client-lawyer relationship, a lawyer may not represent another client except in conformity with this rule. The principles in Rule 1.7 determine whether the interests of the present and former client are adverse. Thus, a lawyer could not properly seek to rescind on behalf of a new client a contract drafted on behalf of the former client. So also a lawyer who has prosecuted an accused person could not properly represent the accused in a subsequent civil action against the government concerning the same transaction.

The scope of a "matter" for purposes of this rule may depend on the facts of a particular situation or transaction. The lawyer's involvement in a matter can also be a question of degree. When a lawyer has been directly involved in a specific transaction, subsequent representation of other clients with materially adverse interests clearly is prohibited. On the other hand, a lawyer who recurrently handled a type of problem for a former client is not precluded from later representing another client in a wholly distinct problem of that type even though the subsequent representation involves a position adverse to the prior client. Similar considerations can apply to the reassignment of military lawyers between defense and prosecution functions within the same military jurisdiction. The underlying question is whether the lawyer was so involved in the matter that the subsequent representation can be justly regarded as a changing of sides in the matter in question.

LAWYERS MOVING BETWEEN FIRMS

When lawyers have been associated in a firm but then end their association, the problem is more complicated. First, the client previously represented must be reasonably assured that the principle of loyalty to the client is not compromised. Second, the rule of disqualification should not be so broadly cast as to preclude other persons from having reasonable choice of legal counsel. Third, the rule of disqualification should not unreasonably hamper lawyers from forming new associations and taking on new clients after having left a previous association. In this connection, it should be recognized that today many lawyers practice in firms, that many, to some degree, limit their practice to one field or another, and that many move from one association to another several times in their careers. If the concept of imputed disqualification were applied with unqualified rigor, the result would be radical curtailment of the opportunity of lawyers to move from one practice setting to another and of the opportunity of clients to change counsel.

Reconciliation of these competing principles in the past has been attempted under two rubrics. One approach has been to seek rules of disqualification per se. For example, it has been held that a partner in a law firm is conclusively presumed to have access to all confidences concerning all clients of the firm. Under this analysis, if a lawyer has been a partner in one law firm and then becomes a partner in another law firm, there is a presumption that all confidences known by a partner in the first firm are known to all partners in the second firm. This presumption might properly be applied in some circumstances, especially where the client has been extensively represented, but may be unrealistic where the client was represented only for limited purposes. Furthermore, such a rigid rule exaggerates the difference between a partner and an associate in modern law firms.

The other rubric formerly used for dealing with vicarious disqualification is the appearance of impropriety proscribed in Canon 9 of the former Michigan Code of Professional Responsibility. Two problems can arise under this rubric. First, the appearance of impropriety might be understood to include any new client-lawyer relationship that might make a former client feel anxious. If that meaning were adopted, disqualification would become little more than a question of subjective judgment by the former client. Second, since "impropriety" is undefined, the term "appearance of impropriety" begs the question. Thus, the problem of imputed disqualification cannot readily be resolved either by simple analogy to a lawyer practicing alone or by the very general concept of appearance of impropriety.

A rule based on a functional analysis is more appropriate for determining the question of vicarious disqualification. Two functions are involved: preserving confidentiality and avoiding positions adverse to a client.

Under Rule 1.10(b), screening may be employed to preserve the confidences of a client when a lawyer has moved from one firm to another. Rule 1.10(b) applies not just to cases in which a lawyer's present and former firms are involved on the date the lawyer moves. The paragraph also applies where the lawyer's present firm later wishes to enter a case from which the lawyer is barred because of information acquired while associated with the prior firm.

CONFIDENTIALITY

Preserving confidentiality is a question of access to information. Access to information, in turn, is essentially a question of fact in particular circumstances. The determination of that question of fact can be aided by inferences, deductions, or assumptions that reasonably may be made about the way in which lawyers work together. A lawyer may have general access to files of all clients of a law firm and may regularly participate in discussions of their affairs; it should be inferred that such a lawyer in fact is privy to all information about all the firm's clients. In contrast, another lawyer may have access to the files of only a limited number of clients and participate in discussion of the affairs of no other clients; in the absence of information to the contrary, it should be inferred that such a lawyer in fact is privy to information about the clients actually served but not those of other clients.

Application of paragraph (b) depends on a situation's particular facts. In any such inquiry, the burden of proof should rest upon the lawyer whose disqualification is sought.

Rule 1.10(b), incorporating paragraph (b) of this rule, operates to disqualify the firm only when the lawyer involved has actual knowledge of information protected by Rules 1.6 and 1.9(c). Thus, if a lawyer while with one firm acquired no knowledge of information relating to a particular client of the firm, and that lawyer later joined another firm, neither the lawyer individually nor the second firm is disqualified from representing another client in the same or a related matter even though the interests of the two clients conflict. See Rule 1.10(c) for the restrictions on a firm once a lawyer has terminated association with the firm.

Independent of the question of disqualification of a firm, a lawyer changing professional association has a continuing duty to preserve confidentiality of information about a client formerly represented. See Rule 1.6.

ADVERSE POSITIONS

The second aspect of loyalty to a client is the lawyer's obligation to decline subsequent representations involving positions adverse to a former client arising in substantially related matters. This obligation requires abstention from adverse representation by the individual lawyer involved, but does not properly entail abstention of other lawyers through imputed disqualification. Thus, if a lawyer left one firm for another, the new affiliation would not preclude the firms involved from continuing to represent clients with adverse interests in the same or related matters, so long as the conditions of Rule 1.10(b) and (c) have been met.

Information acquired by the lawyer in the course of representing a client may not subsequently be used or revealed by the lawyer to the disadvantage of the client. However, the fact that a lawyer has once served a client does not preclude the lawyer from using generally known information about that client when later representing another client.

Disqualification from subsequent representation is for the protection of clients and can be waived by them. A waiver is effective only if there is disclosure of the circumstances, including the lawyer's intended role in behalf of the new client.

With regard to an opposing party raising a question of conflict of interest, see comment to Rule 1.7. With regard to disqualification of a firm with which a lawyer is or was formerly associated, see Rule 1.10.

Rule: 1.10 Imputed Disqualification: General Rule

(a) While lawyers are associated in a firm, none of them shall knowingly represent a client when any one of them practicing alone would be prohibited from doing so by Rules 1.7, 1.8(c), 1.9(a), or 2.2. If a lawyer leaves a firm and becomes associated with another firm, MRPC 1.10(b) governs whether the new firm is imputedly disqualified because of the newly hired lawyer's prior services in or association with the lawyer's former law firm.

(b) When a lawyer becomes associated with a firm, the firm may not knowingly represent a person in the same or a substantially related matter in which that lawyer, or a firm with which the lawyer was associated, is disqualified under Rule 1.9(b), unless:

    (1) the disqualified lawyer is screened from any participation in the matter and is apportioned no part of the fee therefrom; and

(2)   written notice is promptly given to the appropriate tribunal to enable it to ascertain compliance with the provisions of this rule.
(c) When a lawyer has terminated an association with a firm, the firm is not prohibited from thereafter representing a person with interests materially adverse to those of a client represented by the formerly associated lawyer, and not currently represented by the firm, unless:
(1)   the matter is the same or substantially related to that in which the formerly associated lawyer represented the client; and
(2)   any lawyer remaining in the firm has information protected by Rules 1.6 and 1.9(c) that is material to the matter.
(d) A disqualification prescribed by this rule may be waived by the affected client under the conditions stated in Rule 1.7.

Comment

DEFINITION OF "FIRM"

For purposes of these rules, the term "firm" includes lawyers in a private firm and lawyers employed in the legal department of a corporation or other organization or in a legal services organization. Whether two or more lawyers constitute a firm within this definition can depend on the specific facts. For example, two practitioners who share office space and occasionally consult or assist each other ordinarily would not be regarded as constituting a firm. However, if they present themselves to the public in a way suggesting that they are a firm or conduct themselves as a firm, they should be regarded as a firm for purposes of the rules. The terms of any formal agreement between associated lawyers are relevant in determining whether they are a firm, as is the fact that they have mutual access to confidential information concerning the clients they serve. Furthermore, it is relevant in doubtful cases to consider the underlying purpose of the rule that is involved. A group of lawyers could be regarded as a firm for purposes of the rule that the same lawyer should not represent opposing parties in litigation, while it might not be so regarded for purposes of the rule that information acquired by one lawyer is attributed to another.

With respect to the law department of an organization, there is ordinarily no question that the members of the department constitute a firm within the meaning of the Rules of Professional Conduct. However, there can be uncertainty as to the identity of the client. For example, it may not be clear whether the law department of a corporation represents a subsidiary or an affiliated corporation, as well as the corporation by which the members of the department are directly employed. A similar question can arise concerning an unincorporated association and its local affiliates.

Similar questions can also arise with respect to lawyers in legal aid. Lawyers employed in the same unit of a legal service organization constitute a firm, but not necessarily those employed in separate units. As in the case of independent practitioners, whether the lawyers should be treated as being associated with each other can depend on the particular rule that is involved and on the specific facts of the situation.

Where a lawyer has joined a private firm after having represented the government, the situation is governed by Rule 1.11(a) and (b); where a lawyer represents the government after having served private clients, the situation is governed by Rule 1.11(c)(1). The individual lawyer involved is bound by the rules generally, including Rules 1.6, 1.7, and 1.9.

PRINCIPLES OF IMPUTED DISQUALIFICATION
The rule of imputed disqualification stated in paragraph (a) gives effect to the principle of loyalty to the client as it applies to lawyers who practice in a law firm. Such situations can be considered from the premise that a firm of lawyers is essentially one lawyer for purposes of the rules governing loyalty to the client, or from the premise that each lawyer is vicariously bound by the obligation of loyalty owed by each lawyer with whom the lawyer is associated. Paragraph (a) operates only among the lawyers currently associated in a firm. When a lawyer moves or has recently moved from one firm to another, the situation is governed by Rules 1.9(b) and 1.10(b).

Rule 1.10(c) operates to permit a law firm, under certain circumstances, to represent a person with interests directly adverse to those of a client represented by a lawyer who formerly was associated with the firm. The rule applies regardless of when the formerly associated lawyer represented the client. However, the law firm may not represent a person with interests adverse to those of a present client of the firm, which would violate Rule 1.7. Moreover, the firm may not represent the person where the matter is the same or substantially related to that in which the formerly associated lawyer represented the client and any other lawyer currently in the firm has material information protected by Rules 1.6 and 1.9(c), unless the provisions of this rule are followed.

Rule: 1.11 Successive Government and Private Employment

(a) Except as law may otherwise expressly permit, a lawyer shall not represent a private client in connection with a matter in which the lawyer participated personally and substantially as a public officer or employee, unless the appropriate government agency consents after consultation. No lawyer in a firm with which that lawyer is associated may knowingly undertake or continue representation in such a matter, unless:
   (1) the disqualified lawyer is screened from any participation in the matter and is apportioned no part of the fee therefrom; and
   (2) written notice is promptly given to the appropriate government agency to enable it to ascertain compliance with the provisions of this rule.

(b) Except as law may otherwise expressly permit, a lawyer having information that the lawyer knows is confidential government information about a person, acquired when the lawyer was a public officer or employee, may not represent a private client whose interests are adverse to that person in a matter in which the information could be used to the material disadvantage of that person. A firm with which that lawyer is associated may undertake or continue representation in the matter only if the disqualified lawyer is screened from any participation in the matter and is apportioned no part of the fee therefrom.

(c) Except as law may otherwise expressly permit, a lawyer serving as a public officer or employee shall not:

(1) participate in a matter in which the lawyer participated personally and substantially while in private practice or nongovernmental employment, unless under applicable law no one is, or by lawful delegation may be, authorized to act in the lawyer's stead in the matter; or

(2) negotiate for private employment with any person who is involved as a party or as an attorney for a party in a matter in which the lawyer is participating personally and substantially, except that a lawyer serving as a law clerk to a judge, other adjudicative officer, or arbitrator may negotiate for private employment in accordance with Rule 1.12(b).

(d) As used in this rule, the term "matter" includes:

(1) any judicial or other proceeding, application, request for a ruling or other determination, contract, claim, controversy, investigation, charge, accusation, arrest, or other particular matter involving a specific party or parties; and

(2) any other matter covered by the conflict of interest rules of the appropriate government agency.

(e) As used in this rule, the term "confidential government information" means information that has been obtained under governmental authority and that, at the time this rule is applied, the government is prohibited by law from disclosing to the public or has a legal privilege not to disclose, and that is not otherwise available to the public.

Comment

This rule prevents a lawyer from exploiting public office for the advantage of a private client. It is a counterpart of Rule 1.10(b), which applies to lawyers moving from one firm to another.

A lawyer representing a government agency, whether employed or specially retained by the government, is subject to the Rules of Professional Conduct, including the prohibition against representing adverse interests stated in Rule 1.7 and the protections afforded former clients in Rule 1.9. In addition, such a lawyer is subject to Rule 1.11 and to statutes and government regulations regarding conflict of interest. Such statutes and regulations may circumscribe the extent to which the government agency may give consent under this rule.

Where the successive clients are a public agency and a private client, the risk exists that power or discretion vested in public authority might be used for the special benefit of a private client. A lawyer should not be in a position where benefit to a private client might affect performance of the lawyer's professional functions on behalf of public authority. Also, unfair advantage could accrue to the private client by reason of access to confidential government information about the client's adversary obtainable only through the lawyer's government service. However, the rules governing lawyers presently or formerly employed by a government agency should not be so restrictive as to inhibit transfer of employment to and from the government. The government has a legitimate need to attract qualified lawyers as well as to maintain high ethical standards. The provisions for screening and waiver are necessary to prevent the disqualification rule from imposing too severe a deterrent against entering public service.

When the client is an agency of one government, that agency should be treated as a private client for purposes of this rule if the lawyer thereafter represents an agency of another government, as when a lawyer represents a city and subsequently is employed by a federal agency.

Paragraphs (a)(1) and (b) do not prohibit a lawyer from receiving a salary or partnership share established by prior independent agreement. They prohibit directly relating the attorney's compensation to the fee in the matter in which the lawyer is disqualified.

Paragraph (a)(2) does not require that a lawyer give notice to the government agency at a time when premature disclosure would injure the client; a requirement for premature disclosure might preclude engagement of the lawyer. Such notice is, however, required to be given as soon as practicable in order that the government agency will have a reasonable opportunity to ascertain that the lawyer is complying with Rule 1.11 and to take appropriate action if it believes the lawyer is not complying.

Paragraph (b) operates only when the lawyer in question has knowledge of the information, which means actual knowledge; it does not operate with respect to information that merely could be imputed to the lawyer.

Paragraphs (a) and (c) do not prohibit a lawyer from jointly representing a private party and a government agency when doing so is permitted by Rule 1.7 and is not otherwise prohibited by law.

Paragraph (c) does not disqualify other lawyers in the agency with which the lawyer in question has become associated.

Rule: 1.12 Former Judge or Arbitrator

(a) Except as stated in paragraph (d), a lawyer shall not represent anyone in connection with a matter in which the lawyer participated personally and substantially as a judge or other adjudicative officer, arbitrator, or law clerk to such a person, unless all parties to the proceeding consent after consultation.

(b) A lawyer shall not negotiate for employment with any person who is involved as a party, or as an attorney for a party, in a matter in which the lawyer is participating personally and substantially as a judge or other adjudicative officer or arbitrator. A lawyer serving as a law clerk to a judge, other adjudicative officer, or arbitrator may negotiate for employment with a party or attorney involved in a matter in which the clerk is participating personally and substantially, but only after the lawyer has notified the judge, other adjudicative officer, or arbitrator.

(c) If a lawyer is disqualified by paragraph (a), no lawyer in a firm with which that lawyer is associated may knowingly undertake or continue representation in the matter, unless:

    (1) the disqualified lawyer is screened from any participation in the matter and is apportioned no part of the fee therefrom; and

    (2) written notice is promptly given to the appropriate tribunal to enable it to ascertain compliance with the provisions of this rule.

(d) An arbitrator selected as a partisan of a party in a multimember arbitration panel is not prohibited from subsequently representing that party.

Comment

This rule generally parallels Rule 1.11. The term "personally and substantially" signifies that a judge who was a member of a multimember court, and thereafter left judicial office to practice law, is not prohibited from representing a client in a matter pending in the court, but in which the former judge did not participate. So also the fact that a former judge exercised administrative responsibility in a court does not prevent the former judge from acting as a lawyer in a matter where the judge had previously exercised remote or incidental administrative responsibility that did not affect the merits. Compare the comment to Rule 1.11. The term "adjudicative officer" includes such officials as judges pro tempore, referees, special masters, hearing officers and other parajudicial officers, and also lawyers who serve as part-time judges.

Rule: 1.13 Organization as Client

(a) A lawyer employed or retained to represent an organization represents the organization as distinct from its directors, officers, employees, members, shareholders, or other constituents.

(b) If a lawyer for an organization knows that an officer, employee, or other person associated with the organization is engaged in action, intends to act, or refuses to act in a matter related to the representation that is a violation of a legal obligation to the organization, or a violation of law which reasonably might be imputed to the organization, and that is likely to result in substantial injury to the organization, the lawyer shall proceed as is reasonably necessary in the best interest of the organization. In determining how to proceed, the lawyer shall give due consideration to the seriousness of the violation and its consequences, the scope and nature of the lawyer's representation, the responsibility in the organization, and the apparent motivation of the person involved, the policies of the organization concerning such matters, and any other relevant considerations. Any measures taken shall be designed to minimize disruption of the organization and the risk of revealing information relating to the representation to persons outside the organization. Such measures may include among others:

   (1) asking reconsideration of the matter;

   (2) advising that a separate legal opinion on the matter be sought for presentation to appropriate authority in the organization; and

   (3) referring the matter to higher authority in the organization, including, if warranted by the seriousness of the matter, referral to the highest authority that can act in behalf of the organization as determined by applicable law.

(c) When the organization's highest authority insists upon action, or refuses to take action, that is clearly a violation of a legal obligation to the organization or a violation of law which reasonably might be imputed to the organization, and that is likely to result in substantial injury to the organization, the lawyer may take further remedial action that the lawyer reasonably believes to be in the best interest of the organization. Such action may include revealing information otherwise protected by Rule 1.6 only if the lawyer reasonably believes that

   (1) the highest authority in the organization has acted to further the personal or financial interests of members of that authority which are in conflict with the interests of the organization; and

   (2) revealing the information is necessary in the best interest of the organization.

(d) In dealing with an organization's directors, officers, employees, members, shareholders, or other constituents, a lawyer shall explain the identity of the client when the lawyer believes that such explanation is necessary to avoid misunderstandings on their part.

(e) A lawyer representing an organization may also represent any of its directors, officers, employees, members, shareholders, or other constituents, subject to the provisions of Rule 1.7. If the organization's consent to the dual representation is required by Rule 1.7, the consent shall be given by an appropriate official of the organization other than the individual who is to be represented, or by the shareholders.

Comment

THE ENTITY AS THE CLIENT

In transactions with their lawyers, clients who are individuals can speak and decide for themselves, finally and authoritatively. In transactions between an organization and its lawyer, however, the organization can speak and decide only through agents, such as its officers or employees. In effect, the client-lawyer relationship is maintained through an intermediary between the client and the lawyer. This fact requires the lawyer under certain conditions to be concerned whether the intermediary legitimately represents the client.

When officers or employees of the organization make decisions for it, the decisions ordinarily must be accepted by the lawyer even if their utility or prudence is doubtful. Decisions concerning policy and operations, including ones entailing serious risk, are not as such in the lawyer's province. However, different considerations arise when the lawyer knows that the organization may be substantially injured by action of an officer or employee that is in violation of law. In such a circumstance, it may be reasonably necessary for the lawyer to ask the officer, employee, or other agent to reconsider the matter. If that fails, or if the matter is of sufficient seriousness and importance to the organization, it may be reasonably necessary for the lawyer to take steps to have the matter reviewed by a higher authority in the organization. Clear justification should exist for seeking review over the head of the officer or employee normally responsible for it. The stated policy of the organization may define circumstances and prescribe channels for such review, and a lawyer should encourage formulation of such a policy. Even in the absence of organization policy, however, the lawyer may have an obligation to refer a matter to higher authority, depending on the seriousness of the matter and whether the officer in question has apparent motives to act at variance with the organization's interest. Review by the chief executive officer or by the board of directors may be required when the matter is of importance commensurate with their authority. At some point it may be useful or essential to obtain an independent legal opinion.

In an extreme case, it may be reasonably necessary for the lawyer to refer the matter to the organization's highest authority. Ordinarily, that is the board of directors or similar governing body. However, applicable law may prescribe that under certain conditions highest authority reposes elsewhere, for example, in the independent directors of a corporation. The ultimately difficult question is whether the lawyer should be permitted to circumvent the organization's highest authority when it persists in a course of action that is clearly violative of law or a legal obligation to the organization and that is likely to result in substantial injury to the organization.

In such a situation, if the lawyer can take remedial action without a disclosure of information that might adversely affect the organization, the lawyer as a matter of professional discretion may take such actions as the lawyer reasonably believes to be in the best interest of the organization. For example, a lawyer for a close corporation may find it reasonably necessary to disclose misconduct by the board to the shareholders. However, taking such action could entail disclosure of information relating to the representation with consequent risk of injury to the client. When such is the case, the organization is threatened by alternative injuries: the injury that may result from the governing board's action or refusal to act, and the injury that may result if the lawyer's remedial efforts entail disclosure of confidential information. The lawyer may pursue remedial efforts even at the risk of disclosure in the circumstances stated in subparagraphs (c)(1) and (c)(2).

RELATION TO OTHER RULES

The authority and responsibility provided in Rules 1.13(b) and (c) are concurrent with the authority and responsibility provided in other rules. In particular, this rule does not limit the lawyer's authority under Rule 1.6, the responsibilities to the client under Rules 1.8 and 1.16 and the responsibilities of the lawyer under Rule 3.3 or 4.1. If the lawyer's services are being used by an organization to further an illegal act or fraud by the organization, Rule 1.2(c) can be applicable. In connection with complying with Rule 1.2(c), 3.3 or 4.1, or exercising the discretion conferred by Rule 1.6(c), a lawyer for an organization may be in doubt whether the conduct will actually be carried out by the organization. To guide conduct in such circumstances, the lawyer ordinarily should make inquiry within the organization as indicated in Rule 1.13(b).
When the lawyer involved is a member of a firm, the firm's procedures may require referral of difficult questions to a superior in the firm. In that event, Rule 5.2 may be applicable.

UNINCORPORATED ASSOCIATIONS
The duty defined in this rule applies to unincorporated associations.

GOVERNMENTAL AGENCY
The duty defined in this rule applies to governmental organizations. However, when the client is a governmental organization, a different balance may be appropriate between maintaining confidentiality and assuring that the

wrongful official act is prevented or rectified because public business is involved. In addition, duties of lawyers employed by the government or lawyers in military service may be defined by statutes and regulations. Therefore, defining precisely the identity of the client and prescribing the resulting obligations of such lawyers may be more difficult in the government context. In some circumstances, it may be a specific agency, but in others it may be the government as a whole. For example, if the action or failure to act involves the head of a bureau, the department of which the bureau is a part may be the client for purpose of this rule. With these qualifications, the lawyer's substantive duty to the client and reasonable courses of action are essentially the same as when the client is a private organization.

CLARIFYING THE LAWYER'S ROLE

The fact that the organization is the client may be quite unclear to the organization's officials and employees. An organization official accustomed to working with the organization's lawyer may forget that the lawyer represents the organization and not the official. The result of such a misunderstanding can be embarrassing or prejudicial to the individual if, for example, the situation is such that the client-lawyer privilege will not protect the individual's communications to the lawyer. The lawyer should take reasonable care to prevent such consequences. The measures required depend on the circumstances. In routine legal matters, a lawyer for a large corporation does not have to explain to a corporate official that the corporation is the client. On the other hand, if the lawyer is conducting an inquiry involving possible illegal activity, a warning might be essential to prevent unfairness to a corporate employee. See also Rule 4.3.

DUAL REPRESENTATION

Paragraph (e) recognizes that a lawyer for an organization may also represent a principal officer or major shareholder. Such common representation, although often undertaken in practice, can entail serious potential conflicts of interest.

DERIVATIVE ACTIONS

Under generally prevailing law, the shareholders or members of a corporation may bring suit to compel the directors to perform their legal obligations in the supervision of the organization. Members of unincorporated associations have essentially the same right. Such an action may be brought nominally by the organization, but usually is, in fact, a legal controversy over management of the organization.

The question can arise whether counsel for the organization may defend such an action. The proposition that the organization is the lawyer's client does not alone resolve the issue. Most derivative actions are a normal incident of an organization's affairs, to be defended by the organization's lawyer like any other suit. However, if the claim involves serious charges of wrongdoing by those in control of the organization, a conflict may arise between the lawyer's duty to the organization and the lawyer's relationship with the board. In those circumstances, Rule 1.7 governs whether independent counsel should represent the directors.

Rule: 1.14 Client Under a Disability

(a) When a client's ability to make adequately considered decisions in connection with the representation is impaired, whether because of minority or mental disability or for some other reason, the lawyer shall, as far as reasonably possible, maintain a normal client-lawyer relationship with the client.

(b) A lawyer may seek the appointment of a guardian or take other protective action with respect to a client only when the lawyer reasonably believes that the client cannot adequately act in the client's own interest.

Comment

The normal client-lawyer relationship is based on the assumption that the client, when properly advised and assisted, is capable of making decisions about important matters. When the client is a minor or suffers from a mental disorder or disability, however, maintaining the ordinary client-lawyer relationship may not be possible in all respects. In particular, an incapacitated person may have no power to make legally binding decisions. Nevertheless, a client lacking legal competence often has the ability to understand, deliberate upon, and reach conclusions about matters affecting the client's own well-being. Furthermore, to an increasing extent the law recognizes intermediate degrees of competence. For example, children as young as five or six years of age, and certainly those of ten or twelve, are regarded as having opinions that are entitled to weight in legal proceedings concerning their custody. So also, it is recognized that some persons of advanced age can be quite capable of handling routine financial matters while needing special legal protection concerning major transactions.

The fact that a client suffers a disability does not diminish the lawyer's obligation to treat the client with attention and respect. If the person has no guardian or legal representative, the lawyer often must act de facto as guardian. Even if the person does have a legal representative, the lawyer should as far as possible accord the represented person the status of client, particularly in maintaining communication.

If a legal representative has already been appointed for the client, the lawyer should ordinarily look to the representative for decisions on behalf of the client. If a legal representative has not been appointed, the lawyer should see to such an appointment where it would serve the client's best interests. Thus, if a disabled client has substantial property that should be sold for the client's benefit, effective completion of the transaction ordinarily requires appointment of a legal representative. In many circumstances, however, appointment of a legal representative may be expensive or traumatic for the client. Evaluation of these considerations is a matter of professional judgment on the lawyer's part.

If the lawyer represents the guardian as distinct from the ward, and is aware that the guardian is acting adversely to the ward's interest, the lawyer may have an obligation to prevent or rectify the guardian's misconduct. See Rule 1.2(c).

If the lawyer seeks the appointment of a legal representative for the client, the filing of the request itself, together with the facts upon which it is predicated, may constitute the disclosure of confidential information which could be used against the client. If the court to whom the matter is submitted thereafter determines that a legal representative is not necessary, the harm befalling the client as the result of the disclosure may be irreparable. Consequently, consideration should be given to initially filing the petition seeking the appointment of a legal representative ex parte so that the court can decide how best to proceed to minimize the potential adverse consequences to the client by, for example, issuing a protective order limiting the disclosure of the confidential information upon which the request is predicated.

DISCLOSURE OF THE CLIENT'S CONDITION

Rules of procedure in litigation generally provide that minors or persons suffering mental disability shall be represented by a guardian or next friend if they do not have a general guardian. However, disclosure of the client's disability can adversely affect the client's interests. For example, raising the question of disability could, in some circumstances, lead to proceedings for involuntary commitment. The lawyer's position in such cases is an unavoidably difficult one. The lawyer may seek guidance from an appropriate diagnostician.

Rule: 1.15 Safekeeping Property

(a) Definitions.
    (1) "Allowable reasonable fees" for IOLTA accounts are per check charges, per deposit charges, a fee in lieu of a minimum balance, federal deposit insurance fees, sweep fees, and a reasonable IOLTA account administrative or maintenance fee. All other fees are the responsibility of, and may be charged to, the lawyer maintaining the IOLTA account. Fees or charges in excess of the interest or dividends earned on the account for any month or quarter shall not be taken from

interest or dividends earned on other IOLTA accounts or from the principal of the account.

(2) An "eligible institution" for IOLTA accounts is a bank, credit union, or savings and loan association authorized by federal or state law to do business in Michigan, the deposits of which are insured by an agency of the federal government, or is an open-end investment company registered with the Securities and Exchange Commission authorized by federal or state law to do business in Michigan. The eligible institution must pay no less on an IOLTA account than the highest interest rate or dividend generally available from the institution to its non-IOLTA customers when the IOLTA account meets the same minimum balance or other eligibility qualifications. Interest or dividends and fees shall be calculated in accordance with the eligible institution's standard practice, but institutions may elect to pay a higher interest or dividend rate and may elect to waive any fees on IOLTA accounts.

(3) "IOLTA account" refers to an interest- or dividend-bearing account, as defined by the Michigan State Bar Foundation, at an eligible institution from which funds may be withdrawn upon request as soon as permitted by law. An IOLTA account shall include only client or third person funds that cannot earn income for the client or third person in excess of the costs incurred to secure such income while the funds are held.

(4) "Non-IOLTA account" refers to an interest- or dividend-bearing account from which funds may be withdrawn upon request as soon as permitted by law in banks, savings and loan associations, and credit unions authorized by federal or state law to do business in Michigan, the deposits of which are insured by an agency of the federal government. Such an account shall be established as:

 (i) a separate client trust account for the particular client or matter on which the net interest or dividend will be paid to the client or third person, or

 (ii) a pooled client trust account with subaccounting by the bank or savings and loan association or by the lawyer, which will provide for computation of net interest or dividend earned by each client or third person's funds and the payment thereof to the client or third person.

(5) "Lawyer" includes a law firm or other organization with which a lawyer is professionally associated.

(b) A lawyer shall:

(1) promptly notify the client or third person when funds or property in which a client or third person has an interest is received;

(2)   preserve complete records of such account funds and other property for a period of five years after termination of the representation; and

(3)   promptly pay or deliver any funds or other property that the client or third person is entitled to receive, except as stated in this rule or otherwise permitted by law or by agreement with the client or third person, and, upon request by the client or third person, promptly render a full accounting regarding such property.

(c)   When two or more persons (one of whom may be the lawyer) claim interest in the property, it shall be kept separate by the lawyer until the dispute is resolved. The lawyer shall promptly distribute all portions of the property as to which the interests are not in dispute.

(d)   A lawyer shall hold property of clients or third persons in connection with a representation separate from the lawyer's own property. All client or third person funds shall be deposited in an IOLTA or non-IOLTA account. Other property shall be identified as such and appropriately safeguarded.

(e)   In determining whether client or third person funds should be deposited in an IOLTA account or a non-IOLTA account, a lawyer shall consider the following factors:

(1)   the amount of interest or dividends the funds would earn during the period that they are expected to be deposited in light of (a) the amount of the funds to be deposited; (b) the expected duration of the deposit, including the likelihood of delay in the matter for which the funds are held; and (c) the rates of interest or yield at financial institutions where the funds are to be deposited;

(2)   the cost of establishing and administering non-IOLTA accounts for the client or third person's benefit, including service charges or fees, the lawyer's services, preparation of tax reports, or other associated costs;

(3)   the capability of financial institutions or lawyers to calculate and pay income to individual clients or third persons; and

(4)   any other circumstances that affect the ability of the funds to earn a net return for the client or third person.

(f)   A lawyer may deposit the lawyer's own funds in a client trust account only in an amount reasonably necessary to pay financial institution service charges or fees or to obtain a waiver of service charges or fees.

(g)   Legal fees and expenses that have been paid in advance shall be deposited in a client trust account and may be withdrawn only as fees are earned or expenses incurred.

(h)   No interest or dividends from the client trust account shall be available to the lawyer.

(i)   The lawyer shall direct the eligible institution to:

(1) remit the interest and dividends from an IOLTA account, less allowable reasonable fees, if any, to the Michigan State Bar Foundation at least quarterly;

(2) transmit with each remittance a report that shall identify each lawyer for whom the remittance is sent, the amount of remittance attributable to each IOLTA account, the rate and type of interest or dividends applied, the amount of interest or dividends earned, the amount and type of fees deducted, if any, and the average account balance for the period in which the report is made; and

(3) transmit to the depositing lawyer a report in accordance with normal procedures for reporting to its depositors.

(j) A lawyer's good-faith decision regarding the deposit or holding of such funds in an IOLTA account is not reviewable by a disciplinary body. A lawyer shall review the IOLTA account at reasonable intervals to determine whether changed circumstances require the funds to be deposited prospectively in a non-IOLTA account.

Comment

A lawyer should hold property of others with the care required of a professional fiduciary. Securities should be kept in a safe deposit box, except when some other form of safekeeping is warranted by special circumstances. All property which is the property of a client or a third person should be kept separate from the lawyer's business and personal property and, if funds, should be kept in one or more trust accounts. Separate trust accounts may be warranted when administering estate funds or acting in similar fiduciary capacities.

Lawyers often receive from third persons funds from which the lawyer's fee will be paid. If there is risk that the client may divert the funds without paying the fee, the lawyer is not required to remit the portion from which the fee is to be paid. However, a lawyer may not hold funds to coerce a client into accepting the lawyer's contention. The disputed portion of the funds should be kept in trust and the lawyer should suggest means for prompt resolution of the dispute, such as arbitration. The undisputed portion of the funds shall be promptly distributed.

A third person, such as a client's creditors, may have a just claim against funds or other property in a lawyer's custody. A lawyer may have a duty under applicable law to protect such a third-party claim against wrongful interference by the client, and accordingly may refuse to surrender the property to the client. However, a lawyer should not unilaterally assume to arbitrate a dispute between the client and the third person.

The obligations of a lawyer under this rule are independent of those arising from activity other than rendering legal services. For example, a lawyer who serves as an escrow agent is governed by the applicable law relating to fiduciaries even though the lawyer does not render legal services in the transaction.

Rule 1.15A Trust Account Overdraft Notification

(a) Scope. Lawyers who practice law in this jurisdiction shall deposit all funds held in trust in accordance with Rule 1.15. Funds held in trust include funds held in any fiduciary capacity in connection with a representation, whether as trustee, agent, guardian, executor or otherwise.

   (1) "Lawyer" includes a law firm or other organization with which a lawyer is professionally associated.

   (2) For any trust account which is an IOLTA account pursuant to Rule 1.15, the "Notice to Eligible Financial Institution" shall constitute notice to the depository institution that such account is subject to this rule. Lawyers shall clearly identify any other accounts in which funds are held in trust as "trust" or "escrow" accounts, and lawyers must inform the depository institution in writing that such other accounts are trust accounts for the purposes of this rule.

(b) Overdraft Notification Agreement Required. In addition to meeting the requirements of Rule 1.15, each bank, credit union, savings and loan association, savings bank, or open-end investment company registered with the Securities and Exchange Commission (hereinafter "financial institution") referred to in Rule 1.15 must be approved by the State Bar of Michigan in order to serve as a depository for lawyer trust accounts. To apply for approval, financial institutions must file with the State Bar of Michigan a signed agreement, in a form provided by the State Bar of Michigan, that it will submit the reports required in paragraph (d) of this rule to the Grievance Administrator and the trust account holder when any properly payable instrument is presented against a lawyer trust account containing insufficient funds or when any other debit to such account would create a negative balance in the account, whether or not the instrument or other debit is honored and irrespective of any overdraft protection or other similar privileges that may attach to such account. The agreement shall apply to the financial institution for all of its locations in Michigan and cannot be canceled except on 120 days notice in writing to the State Bar of Michigan. Upon notice of cancellation or termination of the agreement, the financial institution must notify all holders of trust accounts subject to the provisions of this rule at least 90 days before termination of approved status that the financial institution will no longer be approved to hold such trust accounts.

(c) The State Bar of Michigan shall establish guidelines regarding the process of approving and terminating "approved status" for financial institutions, and for other operational procedures to effectuate this rule in consultation with the Grievance Administrator. The State Bar of Michigan shall periodically publish a list of approved financial institutions. No trust account shall be maintained in any financial institution that has not been so approved. Approved status under this rule does not substitute for "eligible financial institution" status under Rule 1.15.

(d) Overdraft Reports. The overdraft notification agreement must provide that all reports made by the financial institution contain the following information in a form acceptable to the State Bar of Michigan:

    (1)   The identity of the financial institution

    (2)   The identity of the account holder

    (3)   The account number

    (4)   Information identifying the transaction item

    (5)   The amount and date of the overdraft and either the amount of the returned instrument or other dishonored debit to the account and the date returned or dishonored, or the date of presentation for payment and the date paid.

The financial institution must provide the information required by the notification agreement within five banking days after the date the item was paid or returned unpaid.

(e) Costs. The overdraft notification agreement must provide that a financial institution is not prohibited from charging the lawyer for the reasonable cost of providing the reports and records required by this rule, but those costs may not be charged against principal, nor against interest or dividends earned on trust accounts, including earnings on IOLTA accounts payable to the Michigan State Bar Foundation under Rule 1.15. Such costs, if charged, shall not be borne by clients.

(f) Notification by Lawyers. Every lawyer who receives notification that any instrument presented against the trust account was presented against insufficient funds or that any other debit to such account would create a negative balance in the account, whether or not the instrument or other debit was honored, shall, upon receipt of a request for investigation from the Grievance Administrator, provide the Grievance Administrator, in writing, within 21 days after issuance of such request, a full and fair explanation of the cause of the overdraft and how it was corrected.

(g) Every lawyer practicing or admitted to practice in this jurisdiction shall, as a condition thereof, be conclusively deemed to have consented to the requirements mandated by this rule and shall be deemed to have consented under applicable privacy laws, including but not limited to those of the Gramm-Leach-Bliley Act, 15 USC 6801, to the reporting of information required by this rule.

Rule: 1.16 Declining or Terminating Representation

(a) Except as stated in paragraph (c), a lawyer shall not represent a client or, where representation has commenced, shall withdraw from the representation of a client if:

    (1) the representation will result in violation of the Rules of Professional Conduct or other law;

    (2) the lawyer's physical or mental condition materially impairs the lawyer's ability to represent the client; or

    (3) the lawyer is discharged.

(b) Except as stated in paragraph (c), a lawyer may withdraw from representing a client if withdrawal can be accomplished without material adverse effect on the interests of the client, or if:

    (1) the client persists in a course of action involving the lawyer's services that the lawyer reasonably believes is criminal or fraudulent;

    (2) the client has used the lawyer's services to perpetrate a crime or fraud;

    (3) the client insists upon pursuing an objective that the lawyer considers repugnant or imprudent;

    (4) the client fails substantially to fulfill an obligation to the lawyer regarding the lawyer's services and has been given reasonable warning that the lawyer will withdraw unless the obligation is fulfilled;

    (5) the representation will result in an unreasonable financial burden on the lawyer or has been rendered unreasonably difficult by the client; or

    (6) other good cause for withdrawal exists.

(c) When ordered to do so by a tribunal, a lawyer shall continue representation notwithstanding good cause for terminating the representation.

(d) Upon termination of representation, a lawyer shall take reasonable steps to protect a client's interests, such as giving reasonable notice to the client, allowing time for employment of other counsel, surrendering papers and property to which the client is entitled, and refunding any advance payment of fee that has not been earned. The lawyer may retain papers relating to the client to the extent permitted by law.

Comment

    A lawyer should not accept representation in a matter unless it can be performed competently, promptly, without improper conflict of interest and to completion.

MANDATORY WITHDRAWAL

    A lawyer ordinarily must decline or withdraw from representation if the client demands that the lawyer engage in conduct that is illegal or violates the

Rules of Professional Conduct or other law. The lawyer is not obliged to decline or withdraw simply because the client suggests such a course of conduct; a client may make such a suggestion in the hope that a lawyer will not be constrained by a professional obligation.

When a lawyer has been appointed to represent a client, withdrawal ordinarily requires approval of the appointing authority. See also Rule 6.2. Difficulty may be encountered if withdrawal is based on the client's demand that the lawyer engage in unprofessional conduct. The court may wish an explanation for the withdrawal, while the lawyer may be bound to keep confidential the facts that would constitute such an explanation. The lawyer's statement that professional considerations require termination of the representation ordinarily should be accepted as sufficient.

DISCHARGE

A client has a right to discharge a lawyer at any time, with or without cause, subject to liability for payment for the lawyer's services. Where future dispute about the withdrawal may be anticipated, it may be advisable to prepare a written statement reciting the circumstances.

Whether a client can discharge appointed counsel may depend on applicable law. A client seeking to do so should be given a full explanation of the consequences. These consequences may include a decision by the appointing authority that appointment of successor counsel is unjustified, thus requiring the client to represent himself.

If the client is mentally incompetent, the client may lack the legal capacity to discharge the lawyer, and in any event the discharge may be seriously adverse to the client's interests. The lawyer should make special effort to help the client consider the consequences and, in an extreme case, may initiate proceedings for a conservatorship or similar protection of the client. See Rule 1.14.

OPTIONAL WITHDRAWAL

A lawyer may withdraw from representation in some circumstances. The lawyer has the option to withdraw if it can be accomplished without material adverse effect on the client's interests. Withdrawal is also justified if the client persists in a course of action that the lawyer reasonably believes is illegal or fraudulent, for a lawyer is not required to be associated with such conduct even if the lawyer does not further it. Withdrawal is also permitted if the lawyer's services were misused in the past even if that would materially prejudice the client. The lawyer also may withdraw where the client insists on a repugnant or imprudent objective.

A lawyer may withdraw if the client refuses to abide by the terms of an agreement relating to the representation, such as an agreement concerning fees or court costs, or an agreement limiting the objectives of the representation.

ASSISTING THE CLIENT UPON WITHDRAWAL

Even if the lawyer has been unfairly discharged by the client, a lawyer must take all reasonable steps to mitigate the consequences to the client. The lawyer may retain papers as security for a fee only to the extent permitted by law.

Whether a lawyer for an organization may under certain unusual circumstances have a legal obligation to the organization after withdrawing or being discharged by the organization's highest authority is beyond the scope of these rules.

Rule: 1.17 Sale of a Law Practice

(a) A lawyer or a law firm may sell or purchase a private law practice, including good will, pursuant to this rule.

(b) The fees charged clients shall not be increased by reason of the sale, and a purchaser shall not pass on the cost of good will to a client. The purchaser may, however, refuse to undertake the representation unless the client consents to pay fees regularly charged by the purchaser for rendering substantially similar services to other clients prior to the initiation of the purchase negotiations.

(c) Actual written notice of a pending sale shall be given at least 91 days prior to the date of the sale to each of the seller's clients, and the notice shall include:

   (1) notice of the fact of the proposed sale;

   (2) the identity of the purchaser;

   (3) the terms of any proposed change in the fee agreement permitted under paragraph (b);

   (4) notice of the client's right to retain other counsel or to take possession of the file; and

   (5) notice that the client's consent to the transfer of the client's file to the purchaser will be presumed if the client does not retain other counsel or otherwise object within 90 days of receipt of the notice.

   If the purchaser has identified a conflict of interest that the client cannot waive and that prohibits the purchaser from undertaking the client's matter, the notice shall advise that the client should retain substitute counsel to assume the representation and arrange to have the substitute counsel contact the seller.

(d) If a client cannot be given actual notice as required in paragraph (c), the representation of that client may be transferred to the purchaser only upon entry of an order so authorizing by a judge of the judicial circuit in which the seller maintains the practice. The seller or the purchaser may disclose to the judge in camera information relating to the representation only to the extent necessary to obtain an order authorizing the transfer of a file.

(e) The sale of the good will of a law practice may be conditioned upon the seller ceasing to engage in the private practice of law for a reasonable period of time within the geographical area in which the practice had been conducted.

Comment

This rule permits a selling lawyer or law firm to obtain compensation for the reasonable value of a private law practice in the same manner as withdrawing partners of law firms. See MRPC 5.4 and 5.6. This rule does not apply to the transfer of responsibility for legal representation from one lawyer or firm to another when such transfers are unrelated to the sale of a practice; for transfer of individual files in other circumstances, see MRPC 1.5(e) and 1.16. Admission to or retirement from a law partnership or professional association, retirement plans and similar arrangements, and a sale of tangible assets of a law practice, do not constitute a sale or purchase governed by this rule.

A lawyer participating in the sale of a law practice is subject to the ethical standards that apply when involving another lawyer in the representation of a client. These include, for example, the seller's obligation to act competently in identifying a purchaser qualified to assume the representation of the client and the purchaser's obligation to undertake the representation competently, MRPC 1.1, the obligation to avoid disqualifying conflicts and to secure client consent after consultation for those conflicts that can be waived, MRPC 1.7, and the obligation to protect information relating to the representation, MRPC 1.6 and 1.9.

If approval of the substitution of the purchasing attorney for the selling attorney is required by the rules of any tribunal in which a matter is pending, such approval must be obtained before the matter can be included in the sale, MRPC 1.16. See also MCR 2.117(C).

All the elements of client autonomy, including the client's absolute right to discharge a lawyer and transfer the representation to another, survive the sale of the practice.

SELLING ENTIRE PRACTICE

When a lawyer is closing a private practice, the lawyer may negotiate with a purchaser for the reasonable value of the practice that has been developed by the seller. A seller may agree to transfer matters in one legal field to one purchaser, while transferring matters in another legal field to a separate purchaser. However, a lawyer may not sell individual files piecemeal. A seller closing a practice to accept employment with another firm may take certain matters to the new employer while selling the remainder of the practice.

Although the rule contemplates the sale of substantially all of the law practice, a seller retiring from private practice generally may continue to represent a small number of clients while transferring the balance of the practice.

The seller remains responsible for handling all client matters until the files are transferred under this rule.

TERMINATION OF PRACTICE BY THE SELLER

The rule allows the parties to agree that the seller cease practice in the geographical area for a reasonable time as a condition of the sale. In certain situations, a blanket prohibition on the seller's practice would not be appropriate or warranted, such as a judicial appointee who might subsequently be defeated for reelection, or a seller elected full-time prosecutor. The parties should be allowed to negotiate, for instance, whether any geographical or duration restrictions apply to the seller's employment as a lawyer on the staff of a public agency or of a legal services entity that provides legal services to the poor, or as inside counsel to a business.

CONFLICTS

The practice may be sold to one or more lawyers or firms, provided that the seller assures that all clients are afforded competent representation. Since the number of client matters and their nature directly bear on the valuation of good will and therefore directly relate to selling the law practice, conflicts that cannot be waived by the client and that prevent the prospective purchaser from undertaking the client's matter should be determined promptly. If the purchaser identifies a conflict that the client cannot waive, information should be provided to the client to assist in locating substitute counsel. If the conflict can be waived by the client, the purchaser should explain the implications and determine whether the client consents to the purchaser undertaking the representation. Initial screening with regard to conflicts, for the purpose of determining the good will of the practice, need be no more intrusive than conflict screening of a walk-in prospective client at the purchaser's firm.

CLIENT CONFIDENCES, CONSENT, AND NOTICE

Negotiations between the seller and prospective purchaser prior to disclosure of information relating to a specific representation of an identifiable client can be conducted in a manner that does not violate the confidentiality provisions of MRPC 1.6, just as preliminary discussions are permissible concerning the possible association of another lawyer or mergers between firms, with respect to which client consent is not required. Providing the purchaser access to client-specific information relating to the representation and to the file, however, requires client consent. The rule provides that before such information can be disclosed by the seller to the purchaser the client must be given actual written notice of the fact of the contemplated sale, including the identity of the purchaser, and must be told that the decision to consent or make other arrangements must be made within 90 days. If nothing is heard from the client within that time, consent to the transfer of the client's file to the identified purchaser is presumed.

A lawyer or law firm ceasing to practice cannot be required to remain in practice because some clients cannot be given actual notice of the proposed purchase. Since these clients are not available to consent to the purchase or direct any other disposition of their files, the rule requires an order from a judge of the judicial circuit in which the seller maintains the practice, authorizing their transfer or other disposition. The court can be expected to determine whether reasonable efforts to locate the client have been exhausted, and whether the absent client's legitimate interests will be served by authorizing the transfer of the file so that the purchaser may continue the representation. Preservation of client confidences requires that the petition for a court order be considered in camera.

The client should be told the identity of the purchaser before being asked to consent to disclosure of confidences and secrets or to consent to transfer of the file.

MCR 9.119(G) provides a mechanism for handling client matters when a lawyer dies and there is no one else at the firm to take responsibility for the file.

FEE ARRANGEMENTS BETWEEN CLIENT AND PURCHASER

Paragraph (b) is intended to prohibit a purchaser from charging the former clients of the seller a higher fee than the purchaser is charging the purchaser's existing clients. The sale may not be financed by increases in fees charged the clients of the practice that is purchased. Existing agreements between the seller and the client as to fees and the scope of the work must be honored by the purchaser, unless the client consents after consultation.

Adjustments for differences in the fee schedules of the seller and the purchaser should be made between the seller and purchaser in valuing good will, and not between the client and the purchaser. The purchaser may, however, advise the client that the purchaser will not undertake the representation unless the client consents to pay the higher fees the purchaser usually charges. To prevent client financing of the sale, the higher fee the purchaser may charge must not exceed the fees charged by the purchaser for substantially similar service rendered prior to the initiation of the purchase negotiations.

DECEASED LAWYER

Even though a nonlawyer seller representing the estate of a deceased lawyer is not subject to the Michigan Rules of Professional Conduct, a lawyer who participates in a sale of a law practice must conform to this rule. Therefore, the purchasing lawyer can be expected to see that its requirements are met.

Rules 2.1 - 2.4 Counselor

Rule: 2.1 Advisor

In representing a client, a lawyer shall exercise independent professional judgment and shall render candid advice. In rendering advice, a lawyer may refer not only to law but to other considerations such as moral, economic, social, and political factors that may be relevant to the client's situation.

Comment

SCOPE OF ADVICE

A client is entitled to straightforward advice expressing the lawyer's honest assessment. Legal advice often involves unpleasant facts and alternatives that a client may be disinclined to confront. In presenting advice, a lawyer endeavors to sustain the client's morale and may put advice in as acceptable a form as honesty permits. However, a lawyer should not be deterred from giving candid advice by the prospect that the advice will be unpalatable to the client.

Advice couched in narrowly legal terms may be of little value to a client, especially where practical considerations, such as cost or effects on other people, are predominant. Purely technical legal advice, therefore, can sometimes be inadequate. It is proper for a lawyer to refer to relevant moral and ethical considerations in giving advice. Although a lawyer is not a moral advisor as such, moral and ethical considerations impinge upon most legal questions and may decisively influence how the law will be applied.

A client may expressly or impliedly ask the lawyer for purely technical advice. When such a request is made by a client experienced in legal matters, the lawyer may accept it at face value. When such a request is made by a client inexperienced in legal matters, however, the lawyer's responsibility as advisor may include indicating that more is involved than strictly legal considerations.

Matters that go beyond strictly legal questions may also be in the domain of another profession. Family matters can involve problems within the professional competence of psychiatry, clinical psychology, or social work; business matters can involve problems within the competence of the accounting profession or of financial specialists. Where consultation with a professional in another field is itself something a competent lawyer would recommend, the lawyer should make such a recommendation. At the same time, a lawyer's advice at its best often consists of recommending a course of action in the face of conflicting recommendations of experts.

OFFERING ADVICE

In general, a lawyer is not expected to give advice until asked by the client. However, when a lawyer knows that a client proposes a course of action that is likely to result in substantial adverse legal consequences to the client, the duty to the client under Rule 1.4 may require that the lawyer act if the client's course of action is related to the representation. A lawyer ordinarily has no duty to initiate investigation of a client's affairs or to give advice that the client has indicated is unwanted, but a lawyer may initiate advice to a client when doing so appears to be in the client's interest.

Rule: 2.2 Intermediary

(a) A lawyer may act as intermediary between clients if:
   (1) the lawyer consults with each client concerning the implications of the common representation, including the advantages and risks involved and the effect on the client-lawyer privileges, and obtains each client's consent to the common representation;
   (2) the lawyer reasonably believes that the matter can be resolved on terms compatible with the clients' best interests, that each client will be able to make adequately informed decisions in the matter, and that there is little risk of material prejudice to the interests of any of the clients if the contemplated resolution is unsuccessful; and
   (3) the lawyer reasonably believes that the common representation can be undertaken impartially and without improper effect on other responsibilities the lawyer has to any of the clients.
(b) While acting as intermediary, the lawyer shall consult with each client concerning the decisions to be made and the considerations relevant in making them, so that each client can make adequately informed decisions.
(c) A lawyer shall withdraw as intermediary if any of the clients so requests, or if any of the conditions stated in paragraph (a) is no longer satisfied. Upon withdrawal, the lawyer shall not continue to represent any of the clients in the matter that was the subject of the intermediation.

Comment

A lawyer acts as intermediary under this rule when the lawyer represents two or more parties with potentially conflicting interests. A key factor in defining the relationship is whether the parties share responsibility for the lawyer's fee, but the common representation may be inferred from other circumstances. Because confusion can arise as to the lawyer's role where each party is not separately represented, it is important that the lawyer make clear the relationship.

The rule does not apply to a lawyer acting as arbitrator or mediator between or among parties who are not clients of the lawyer, even where the lawyer has been appointed with the concurrence of the parties. In performing such a role the lawyer may be subject to applicable codes of ethics, such as the Code of Ethics for Arbitration in Commercial Disputes prepared by a joint committee of the American Bar Association and the American Arbitration Association.

A lawyer acts as intermediary in seeking to establish or adjust a relationship between clients on an amicable and mutually advantageous basis, for example, in helping to organize a business in which two or more clients are entrepreneurs, working out the financial reorganization of an enterprise in which two or more clients have an interest, arranging a property distribution in settlement of an estate, or mediating a dispute between clients. The lawyer seeks to resolve potentially conflicting interests by developing the parties' mutual interests. The alternative can be that each party may have to obtain separate representation, with the possibility in some situations of incurring additional cost, complication, or even litigation. Given these and other relevant factors, all the clients may prefer that the lawyer act as intermediary.

In considering whether to act as intermediary between clients, a lawyer should be mindful that if the intermediation fails the result can be additional cost, embarrassment, and recrimination. In some situations the risk of failure is so great that intermediation is plainly impossible. For example, a lawyer cannot undertake common representation of clients between whom contentious litigation is imminent or who contemplate contentious negotiations. More generally, if the relationship between the parties has already assumed definite antagonism, the possibility that the clients' interests can be adjusted by intermediation ordinarily is not very good.

The appropriateness of intermediation can depend on its form. Forms of intermediation include informal arbitration (where each client's case is presented by the respective client and the lawyer decides the outcome), mediation, and common representation where the clients' interests are substantially, though not entirely, compatible. One form may be appropriate in circumstances where another would not. Other relevant factors are whether the lawyer subsequently will represent both parties on a continuing basis and whether the situation involves creating a relationship between the parties or terminating one.

CONFIDENTIALITY AND PRIVILEGE

A particularly important factor in determining the appropriateness of intermediation is the effect on client-lawyer confidentiality and the client-lawyer privilege. In a common representation, the lawyer is still required both to keep each client adequately informed and to maintain confidentiality of information relating to the representation. See Rules 1.4 and 1.6. Complying with both requirements while acting as intermediary requires a delicate balance. If the balance cannot be maintained, the common representation is improper. With regard to the client-lawyer privilege, the prevailing rule is that as between commonly represented clients the privilege does not attach. Hence, it must be assumed that if litigation eventuates between the clients, the privilege will not protect any such communications, and the clients should be so advised.

Since the lawyer is required to be impartial between commonly represented clients, intermediation is improper when that impartiality cannot be maintained. For example, a lawyer who has represented one of the clients for a long period and in a variety of matters might have difficulty being impartial between that client and one to whom the lawyer has only recently been introduced.

CONSULTATION

In acting as intermediary between clients, the lawyer is required to consult with the clients on the implications of doing so, and proceed only upon consent based on such a consultation. The consultation should make clear that the lawyer's role is not that of partisanship normally expected in other circumstances.

Paragraph (b) is an application of the principle expressed in Rule 1.4. Where the lawyer is intermediary, the clients ordinarily must assume greater responsibility for decisions than when each client is independently represented.

WITHDRAWAL

Common representation does not diminish the rights of each client in the client-lawyer relationship. Each has the right to loyal and diligent representation, the right to discharge the lawyers stated in Rule 1.16, and the protection of Rule 1.9 concerning obligations to a former client.

Rule: 2.3 Evaluation for Use by Third Persons

(a) A lawyer may, for the use of someone other than the client, undertake an evaluation of a matter affecting a client if:
  (1) the lawyer reasonably believes that making the evaluation is compatible with other aspects of the lawyer's relationship with the client; and
  (2) the client consents after consultation.
(b) Except as disclosure is required in connection with a report of an evaluation, information relating to the evaluation is protected by Rule 1.6.

Comment

DEFINITION

An evaluation may be performed at the client's direction, but for the primary purpose of establishing information for the benefit of third parties; for example, an opinion concerning the title of property rendered at the behest of a vendor for the information of a prospective purchaser, or at the behest of a borrower for the information of a prospective lender. In some situations, the evaluation may be required by a government agency, for example, an opinion concerning the legality of the securities registered for sale under the securities laws. In other instances, the evaluation may be required by a third person, such as a purchaser of a business.

Lawyers for the government may be called upon to give a formal opinion on the legality of contemplated government agency action. In making such an evaluation, the government lawyer acts at the behest of the government as the client, but for the purpose of establishing the limits of the agency's authorized activity. Such an opinion is to be distinguished from confidential legal advice given agency officials. The critical question is whether the opinion is to be made public.

A legal evaluation should be distinguished from an investigation of a person with whom the lawyer does not have a client-lawyer relationship. For example, a lawyer retained by a purchaser to analyze a vendor's title to property does not have a client-lawyer relationship with the vendor. So also, an investigation into a person's affairs by a government lawyer, or by special counsel employed by the government, is not an evaluation as that term is used in this rule. The question is whether the lawyer is retained by the person whose affairs are being examined. When the lawyer is retained by that person, the general rules concerning loyalty to client and preservation of confidences apply, which is not the case if the lawyer is retained by someone else. For this reason, it is essential to identify the person by whom the lawyer is retained. This should be made clear not only to the person under examination, but also to others to whom the results are to be made available.

DUTY TO THIRD PERSON

When the evaluation is intended for the information or use of a third person, a legal duty to that person may or may not arise. That legal question is beyond the scope of this rule. However, since such an evaluation involves a departure from the normal client-lawyer relationship, careful analysis of the situation is required. The lawyer must be satisfied as a matter of professional judgment that making the evaluation is compatible with other functions undertaken in behalf of the client. For example, if the lawyer is acting as advocate in defending the client against charges of fraud, it would normally be incompatible with that responsibility for the lawyer to perform an evaluation for others concerning the same or a related transaction. Assuming no such impediment is apparent, however, the lawyer should advise the client of the implications of the evaluation, particularly the lawyer's responsibilities to third persons and the duty to disseminate the findings.

ACCESS TO AND DISCLOSURE OF INFORMATION

The quality of an evaluation depends on the freedom and extent of the investigation upon which it is based. Ordinarily a lawyer should have whatever latitude of investigation seems necessary as a matter of professional judgment. Under some circumstances, however, the terms of the evaluation may be limited. For example, certain issues or sources may be categorically excluded, or the scope of search may be limited by time constraints or the noncooperation of persons having relevant information. Any such limitations which are material to the evaluation should be described in the report. If after a lawyer has commenced an evaluation the client refuses to comply with the terms upon which it was understood the evaluation was to have been made, the lawyer's obligations are determined by law, having reference to the terms of the client's agreement and the surrounding circumstances.

FINANCIAL AUDITORS' REQUESTS FOR INFORMATION

When a question concerning the legal situation of a client arises at the instance of the client's financial auditor and the question is referred to the lawyer, the lawyer's response may be made in accordance with procedures recognized in the legal profession. Such a procedure is set forth in the American Bar Association Statement of Policy Regarding Lawyers' Responses to Auditors' Requests for Information, adopted in 1975.

Rule 2.4 Lawyer Serving as Third-Party Neutral

(a) A lawyer serves as a third-party neutral when the lawyer assists two or more persons who are not clients of the lawyer to reach a resolution of a dispute or other matter that has arisen between them. Service as a third-party neutral may include service as an arbitrator, a mediator, or in such other capacity as will enable the lawyer to assist the parties to resolve the matter.

(b) A lawyer serving as a third-party neutral must inform unrepresented parties that the lawyer is not representing them. When the lawyer knows or reasonably should know that a party does not understand the lawyer's role in the matter, the lawyer must explain the difference between the lawyer's role as a third-party neutral and a lawyer's role as one who represents a client.

Comment

Alternative dispute resolution has become a substantial part of the civil justice system. Aside from representing clients in dispute-resolution processes, lawyers often serve as third-party neutrals. A third-party neutral is a person, such as a mediator, an arbitrator, a conciliator, or an evaluator, who assists the parties, represented or unrepresented, in the resolution of a dispute or in the arrangement of a transaction. Whether a third-party neutral serves primarily as a facilitator, an evaluator, or a decision maker depends on the particular process that is selected by the parties or mandated by a court.

The role of a third-party neutral is not unique to lawyers, although, in some court-connected contexts, only lawyers are allowed to serve in this role or to handle certain types of cases. In performing this role, the lawyer may be subject to court rules or other law that apply either to third-party neutrals generally or to lawyers serving as third-party neutrals. Lawyer-neutrals also may be subject to various codes of ethics, such as the Code of Ethics for Arbitration in Commercial Disputes prepared by a joint committee of the American Bar Association and the American Arbitration Association, or the Model Standards of Conduct for Mediators jointly prepared by the American Bar Association, the American Arbitration Association, and the Society of Professionals in Dispute Resolution.

Unlike nonlawyers who serve as third-party neutrals, lawyers serving in this role may experience unique problems as a result of differences between the role of a third-party neutral and a lawyer's service as a client representative. The potential for confusion is significant when the parties are unrepresented in the process. Thus, paragraph (b) requires a lawyer-neutral to inform unrepresented parties that the lawyer is not representing them. For some parties, particularly parties who frequently use dispute-resolution processes, this information will be sufficient. For others, particularly those who are using the process for the first time, more information will be required. Where appropriate, the lawyer should inform unrepresented parties of the important differences between the lawyer's role as third-party neutral and a lawyer's role as a client representative, including the inapplicability of the attorney-client evidentiary privilege. The extent of disclosure required under this paragraph will depend on the particular parties involved and the subject matter of the proceeding, as well as the particular features of the dispute-resolution process selected.

A lawyer who serves as a third-party neutral subsequently may be asked to serve as a lawyer representing a client in the same matter. The conflicts of interest that arise for both the individual lawyer and the lawyer's law firm are addressed in Rule 1.12.

Lawyers who represent clients in alternative dispute resolution are governed by the Michigan Rules of Professional Conduct. When the dispute-resolution process takes place before a tribunal, as in binding arbitration, the lawyer's duty of candor is governed by Rule 3.3. Otherwise, the lawyer's duty of candor toward both the third-party neutral and other parties is governed by Rule 4.1.

Rules 3.1 - 3.9 Advocate

Rule: 3.1 Meritorious Claims and Contentions

A lawyer shall not bring or defend a proceeding, or assert or controvert an issue therein, unless there is a basis for doing so that is not frivolous. A lawyer may offer a good-faith argument for an extension, modification, or reversal of existing law. A lawyer for the defendant in a criminal proceeding, or the respondent in a proceeding that could result in incarceration, may so defend the proceeding as to require that every element of the case be established.

Comment

The advocate has a duty to use legal procedure for the fullest benefit of the client's cause, but also has a duty not to abuse legal procedure. The law, both procedural and substantive, establishes the limits within which an advocate may proceed. However, the law is not always clear and never is static. Accordingly, in determining the proper scope of advocacy, account must be taken of the law's ambiguities and potential for change.

The filing of an action or defense or similar action taken for a client is not frivolous merely because the facts have not first been fully substantiated or because the lawyer expects to develop vital evidence only by discovery. What is required of lawyers is that they inform themselves about the facts of their clients' cases and the applicable law and determine that they can make good-faith arguments in support of their clients' positions. Such action is not frivolous even though the lawyer believes that the client's position ultimately will not prevail. The action is frivolous, however, if the lawyer is unable either to make a good-faith argument on the merits of the action taken or to support the action taken by a good-faith argument for an extension, modification, or reversal of existing law.

Rule: 3.2 Expediting Litigation

A lawyer shall make reasonable efforts to expedite litigation consistent with the interests of the client.

Although a judge bears the responsibility of assuring the progress of a court's docket, dilatory practices by a lawyer can bring the administration of justice into disrepute. Delay should not be indulged merely for the convenience of the advocates, or for the purpose of frustrating an opposing party's attempt to obtain rightful redress or repose. It is not a justification that similar conduct is often tolerated by the bench and bar. Even though it causes delay, a course of action is proper if a competent lawyer acting in good faith would regard the course of action as having some substantial purpose other than delay. Realizing financial or other benefit from otherwise improper delay in litigation is not a legitimate interest of the client.

Rule: 3.3 Candor Toward the Tribunal

(a) A lawyer shall not knowingly:
    (1) make a false statement of material fact or law to a tribunal or fail to correct a false statement of material fact or law previously made to the tribunal by the lawyer;
    (2) fail to disclose to a tribunal controlling legal authority in the jurisdiction known to the lawyer to be directly adverse to the position of the client and not disclosed by opposing counsel; or
    (3) offer evidence that the lawyer knows to be false. If a lawyer has offered material evidence and comes to know of its falsity, the lawyer shall take reasonable remedial measures, including, if necessary, disclosure to the tribunal

(b) If a lawyer knows that the lawyer's client or other person intends to engage, is engaging, or has engaged in criminal or fraudulent conduct related to an adjudicative proceeding involving the client, the lawyer shall take reasonable remedial measures, including, if necessary, disclosure to the tribunal.

(c) The duties stated in paragraphs (a) and (b) continue to the conclusion of the proceeding, and apply even if compliance requires disclosure of information otherwise protected by Rule 1.6.

(d) In an ex parte proceeding, a lawyer shall inform the tribunal of all material facts that are known to the lawyer and that will enable the tribunal to make an informed decision, whether or not the facts are adverse.

(e) When false evidence is offered, a conflict may arise between the lawyer's duty to keep the client's revelations confidential and the duty of candor to the court. Upon ascertaining that material evidence is false, the lawyer should seek to persuade the client that the evidence should not be offered or, if it has been offered, that its false character should immediately be

Rule: 3.3 Candor Toward the Tribunal

disclosed. If the persuasion is ineffective, the lawyer must take reasonable remedial measures. The advocate should seek to withdraw if that will remedy the situation. If withdrawal from the representation is not permitted or will not remedy the effect of the false evidence, the lawyer must make such disclosure to the tribunal as is reasonably necessary to remedy the situation, even if doing so requires the lawyer to reveal information that otherwise would be protected by Rule 1.6.

Comment

This rule governs the conduct of a lawyer who is representing a client in a tribunal. It also applies when the lawyer is representing a client in an ancillary proceeding conducted pursuant to the tribunal's adjudicative authority, such as a deposition. Thus, subrule (a) requires a lawyer to take reasonable remedial measures if the lawyer comes to know that a client who is testifying in a deposition has offered evidence that is false.

As officers of the court, lawyers have special duties to avoid conduct that undermines the integrity of the adjudicative process. A lawyer acting as an advocate in an adjudicative proceeding has an obligation to present the client's case with persuasive force. Performance of that duty while maintaining confidences of the client is qualified, however, by the advocate's duty of candor to the tribunal. . Consequently, although a lawyer in an adversary proceeding is not required to present an impartial exposition of the law or to vouch for the evidence submitted in a cause, the lawyer must not allow the tribunal to be misled by false statements of law or fact or evidence that the lawyer knows to be false.

REPRESENTATIONS BY A LAWYER

An advocate is responsible for pleadings and other documents prepared for litigation, but is usually not required to have personal knowledge of matters asserted therein, because litigation documents ordinarily present assertions by the client or by someone on the client's behalf and not assertions by the lawyer. Compare Rule 3.1. However, an assertion purporting to be on the lawyer's own knowledge, as in an affidavit by the lawyer or in a statement in open court, may properly be made only when the lawyer knows the assertion is true or believes it to be true on the basis of a reasonably diligent inquiry. There are circumstances where failure to make a disclosure is the equivalent of an affirmative misrepresentation. The obligation prescribed in Rule 1.2(c) not to counsel a client to commit or assist the client in committing a fraud applies in litigation. Regarding compliance with Rule 1.2(c), see the comment to that rule. See also the comment to Rule 8.4(b).

LEGAL ARGUMENT

Legal argument based on a knowingly false representation of law constitutes dishonesty toward the tribunal. A lawyer is not required to make a disinterested exposition of the law, but must recognize the existence of pertinent legal authorities. Furthermore, as stated in paragraph (a)(2), an advocate has a duty to disclose directly controlling adverse authority that has not been disclosed by the opposing party. The underlying concept is that legal argument is a discussion seeking to determine the legal premises properly applicable to the case.

OFFERING EVIDENCE

Paragraph (a)(3) requires that a lawyer refuse to offer evidence that the lawyer knows to be false, regardless of the client's wishes. This duty is premised on the lawyer's obligation as an officer of the court to prevent the trier of fact from being misled by false evidence. A lawyer does not violate this rule if the lawyer offers the evidence for the purpose of establishing its falsity.

If a lawyer knows that the client intends to testify falsely or wants the lawyer to introduce false evidence, the lawyer should seek to persuade the client that the evidence should not be offered. If the persuasion is ineffective and the lawyer continues to represent the client, the lawyer must refuse to offer the false evidence. If only a portion of a witness' testimony will be false, the lawyer may call the witness to testify but may not elicit or otherwise permit the witness to present the testimony that the lawyer knows is false. A lawyer's knowledge that evidence is false can be inferred from the circumstances. Thus, although a lawyer should resolve doubts about the veracity of testimony or other evidence in favor of the client, the lawyer cannot ignore an obvious falsehood.

REMEDIAL MEASURES

Having offered material evidence in the belief that it was true, a lawyer may subsequently come to know that the evidence is false. Or a lawyer may be surprised when the lawyer's client, or another witness called by the lawyer, offers testimony the lawyer knows to be false, either during the lawyer's direct examination or in response to cross-examination by the opposing lawyer. In such situations, or if the lawyer knows of the falsity of testimony elicited from the client during a deposition, the lawyer must take reasonable remedial measures. If that fails, the lawyer must take further remedial action. It is for the tribunal then to determine what should be done—making a statement about the matter to the trier of fact, ordering a mistrial, or perhaps nothing

The disclosure of a client's false testimony can result in grave consequences to the client, including a sense of betrayal, the loss of the case, or perhaps a prosecution for perjury. However, the alternative is that the lawyer aids in the deception of the court, thereby subverting the truth-finding process that the adversarial system is designed to implement. See Rule 1.2(c). Furthermore, unless it is clearly understood that the lawyer must remediate the disclosure of false evidence, the client could simply reject the lawyer's counsel to reveal the false evidence and require that the lawyer remain silent. Thus, the client could insist that the lawyer assist in perpetrating a fraud on the court.

PRESERVING INTEGRITY OF ADJUDICATIVE PROCESS

Lawyers have a special obligation to protect a tribunal against criminal or fraudulent conduct that undermines the integrity of the adjudicative process, such as bribing, intimidating, or otherwise unlawfully communicating with a witness, juror, court official, or other participant in the proceeding, unlawfully destroying or concealing documents or other evidence, or failing to disclose information to the tribunal when required by law to do so. Thus, paragraph (b) requires a lawyer to take reasonable remedial measures, including disclosure, if necessary, whenever the lawyer knows that a person, including the lawyer's client, intends to engage, is engaging, or has engaged in criminal or fraudulent conduct related to the proceeding. See Rule 3.4.

DURATION OF OBLIGATION

A practical time limit on the obligation to rectify the presentation of false evidence or false statements of law and fact must be established. The conclusion of the proceeding is a reasonably definite point for the termination of the obligation.

EX PARTE PROCEEDINGS

Ordinarily, an advocate has the limited responsibility of presenting one side of the matters that a tribunal should consider in reaching a decision; the conflicting position is expected to be presented by the opposing party. However, in an ex parte proceeding, such as an application for a temporary restraining order, there is no balance of presentation by opposing advocates. The object of an ex parte proceeding is nevertheless to yield a substantially just result. The judge has an affirmative responsibility to accord the absent party just consideration. The lawyer for the represented party has the correlative duty to make disclosures of material facts that are known to the lawyer and that the lawyer reasonably believes are necessary to an informed decision.

WITHDRAWAL

Normally, a lawyer's compliance with the duty of candor imposed by this rule does not require that the lawyer withdraw from the representation of a client whose interests will be or have been adversely affected by the lawyer's disclosure. The lawyer may, however, be required by Rule 1.16(a) to seek permission of the tribunal to withdraw if the lawyer's compliance with this rule's duty of candor results in such an extreme deterioration of the client-lawyer relationship that the lawyer can no longer competently represent the client. Also see Rule 1.16(b) for the circumstances in which a lawyer will be permitted to seek a tribunal's permission to withdraw. In connection with a request for permission to withdraw that is premised on a client's misconduct, a lawyer may reveal information relating to the representation only to the extent reasonably necessary to comply with this rule or as otherwise permitted by Rule 1.6.

Rule: 3.4 Fairness to Opposing Party and Counsel

A lawyer shall not:

(a) unlawfully obstruct another party's access to evidence; unlawfully alter, destroy, or conceal a document or other material having potential evidentiary value; or counsel or assist another person to do any such act;

(b) falsify evidence, counsel or assist a witness to testify falsely, or offer an inducement to a witness that is prohibited by law;

(c) knowingly disobey an obligation under the rules of a tribunal except for an open refusal based on an assertion that no valid obligation exists;

(d) in pretrial procedure, make a frivolous discovery request or fail to make reasonably diligent efforts to comply with a legally proper discovery request by an opposing party;

(e) during trial, allude to any matter that the lawyer does not reasonably believe is relevant or that will not be supported by admissible evidence, assert personal knowledge of facts in issue except when testifying as a witness, or state a personal opinion as to the justness of a cause, the credibility of a witness, the culpability of a civil litigant, or the guilt or innocence of an accused; or

(f) request a person other than a client to refrain from voluntarily giving relevant information to another party, unless:

  (1) the person is an employee or other agent of a client for purposes of MRE 801(d)(2)(D); and

  (2) the lawyer reasonably believes that the person's interests will not be adversely affected by refraining from giving such information.

Comment

The procedure of the adversary system contemplates that the evidence in a case is to be marshaled competitively by the contending parties. Fair competition in the adversary system is secured by prohibitions against destruction or concealment of evidence, improper influence of witnesses, obstructive tactics in discovery procedure, and the like.

Documents and other items of evidence are often essential to establish a claim or defense. Subject to evidentiary privileges, the right of an opposing party, including the government, to obtain evidence through discovery or subpoena is an important procedural right. The exercise of that right can be frustrated if relevant material is altered, concealed or destroyed. Other law makes it an offense to destroy material for purpose of impairing its availability in a pending proceeding or one whose commencement can be foreseen. Falsifying evidence is also generally a criminal offense. Paragraph (a) applies to evidentiary material generally, including computerized information.

With regard to paragraph (b), it is not improper to pay a witness' expenses or to compensate an expert witness on terms permitted by law. It is, however, improper to pay an occurrence witness any fee for testifying beyond that authorized by law, and it is improper to pay an expert witness a contingent fee.

Rule: 3.5 Impartiality and Decorum of the Tribunal

A lawyer shall not:
(a) seek to influence a judge, juror, prospective juror, or other official by means prohibited by law;
(b) communicate ex parte with such a person concerning a pending matter, unless authorized to do so by law or court order;
(c) communicate with a juror or prospective juror after discharge of the jury if:
   (1) the communication is prohibited by law or court order;
   (2) the juror has made known to the lawyer a desire not to communicate; or
   (3) the communication constitutes misrepresentation, coercion, duress or harassment; or
(d) engage in undignified or discourteous conduct toward the tribunal.

Comment

Many forms of improper influence upon a tribunal are proscribed by criminal law. Others are specified in the Michigan Code of Judicial Conduct, with which an advocate should be familiar. A lawyer is required to avoid contributing to a violation of such provisions.

During a proceeding a lawyer may not communicate ex parte with persons serving in an official capacity in the proceeding, such as judges, masters, or jurors, unless authorized to do so by law or court order.

A lawyer may on occasion want to communicate with a juror or prospective juror after the jury has been discharged. The lawyer may do so, unless the communication is prohibited by law or a court order, but must respect the desire of the juror not to talk with the lawyer. The lawyer may not engage in improper conduct during the communication.

The advocate's function is to present evidence and argument so that the cause may be decided according to law. Refraining from undignified or discourteous conduct is a corollary of the advocate's right to speak on behalf of litigants. A lawyer may stand firm against abuse by a judge, but should avoid reciprocation; the judge's default is no justification for similar dereliction by an advocate. An advocate can present the cause, protect the record for subsequent review, and preserve professional integrity by patient firmness no less effectively than by belligerence or theatrics.

Rule: 3.6 Trial Publicity

(a) A lawyer who is participating or has participated in the investigation or litigation of a matter shall not make an extrajudicial statement that the lawyer knows or reasonably should know will be disseminated by means of public communication and will have a substantial likelihood of materially prejudicing an adjudicative proceeding in the matter A statement is likely to have a substantial likelihood of materially prejudicing an adjudicative proceeding when it refers to a civil matter triable to a jury, a criminal matter, or any other proceeding that could result in incarceration, and the statement relates to:

   (1) the character, credibility, reputation, or criminal record of a party, of a suspect in a criminal investigation or of a witness, or the identity of a witness, or the expected testimony of a party or witness;

   (2) in a criminal case or proceeding that could result in incarceration, the possibility of a plea of guilty to the offense or the existence or contents of any confession, admission, or statement given by a defendant or suspect, or that person's refusal or failure to make a statement;

   (3) the performance or results of any examination or test, or the refusal or failure of a person to submit to an examination or test, or the identity or nature of physical evidence expected to be presented;

   (4) any opinion as to the guilt or innocence of a defendant or suspect in a criminal case or proceeding that could result in incarceration;

   (5) information that the lawyer knows or reasonably should know is likely to be inadmissible as evidence in a trial and that would, if disclosed, create a substantial risk of prejudicing an impartial trial; or

   (6) the fact that a defendant has been charged with a crime, unless there is included therein a statement explaining that the charge is merely an accusation and that the defendant is presumed innocent until and unless proven guilty.

(b) Notwithstanding paragraph (a), a lawyer who is participating or has participated in the investigation or litigation of a matter may state without elaboration:

(1)   the nature of the claim, offense, or defense involved;

(2)   information contained in a public record;

(3)   that an investigation of a matter is in progress;

(4)   the scheduling or result of any step in litigation;

(5)   a request for assistance in obtaining evidence and information necessary thereto;

(6)   a warning of danger concerning the behavior of a person involved, when there is reason to believe that there exists the likelihood of substantial harm to an individual or to the public interest; and

(7)   in a criminal case, also:

    (i)   the identity, residence, occupation, and family status of the accused;

    (ii)   if the accused has not been apprehended, information necessary to aid in apprehension of that person;

    (iii) the fact, time and place of arrest; and

    (iv) the identity of investigating and arresting officers or agencies and the length of the investigation.

(c) No lawyer associated in a firm or government agency with a lawyer subject to paragraph (a) shall make a statement prohibited by paragraph (a).

Comment

It is difficult to strike a balance between protecting the right to a fair trial and safeguarding the right of free expression. Preserving the right to a fair trial necessarily entails some curtailment of the information that may be disseminated about a party before trial, particularly where trial by jury is involved. If there were no such limits, the result would be the practical nullification of the protective effect of the rules of forensic decorum and the exclusionary rules of evidence. On the other hand, there are vital social interests served by the free dissemination of information about events having legal consequences and about legal proceedings themselves. The public has a right to know about threats to its safety and measures aimed at assuring its security. It also has a legitimate interest in the conduct of judicial proceedings, particularly in matters of general public concern. Furthermore, the subject matter of legal proceedings is often of direct significance in debate and deliberation over questions of public policy.

Special rules of confidentiality may validly govern juvenile, domestic relations, and mental disability proceedings, in addition to other types of litigation. Rule 3.4(c) requires compliance with such rules.

Rule 3.6 sets forth a basic general prohibition against a lawyer's making statements that the lawyer knows or should know will have a substantial likelihood of materially prejudicing an adjudicative proceeding. Recognizing that the public value of informed commentary is great and the likelihood of prejudice to a proceeding by the commentary of a lawyer who is not involved in the proceeding is small, the rule applies only to lawyers who are, or who have been, involved in the investigation or litigation of a case, and their associates.

See Rule 3.8(e) for additional duties of prosecutors in connection with extrajudicial statements about criminal proceedings.

Rule: 3.7 Lawyer as Witness

(a) A lawyer shall not act as advocate at a trial in which the lawyer is likely to be a necessary witness except where:
  (1) the testimony relates to an uncontested issue;
  (2) the testimony relates to the nature and value of legal services rendered in the case; or
  (3) disqualification of the lawyer would work substantial hardship on the client.
(b) A lawyer may act as advocate in a trial in which another lawyer in the lawyer's firm is likely to be called as a witness unless precluded from doing so by Rule 1.7 or Rule 1.9.

Comment

Combining the roles of advocate and witness can prejudice the opposing party and can involve a conflict of interest between the lawyer and client.

The opposing party may properly object where the combination of roles may prejudice that party's rights in the litigation. A witness is required to testify on the basis of personal knowledge, while an advocate is expected to explain and comment on evidence given by others. It may not be clear whether a statement by an advocate-witness should be taken as proof or as an analysis of the proof.

Paragraph (a)(1) recognizes that if the testimony will be uncontested, the ambiguities in the dual role are purely theoretical. Paragraph (a)(2) recognizes that where the testimony concerns the extent and value of legal services rendered in the action in which the testimony is offered, permitting the lawyers to testify avoids the need for a second trial with new counsel to resolve that issue. Moreover, in such a situation the judge has firsthand knowledge of the matter in issue; hence, there is less dependence on the adversary process to test the credibility of the testimony.

Apart from these two exceptions, paragraph (a)(3) recognizes that a balancing is required between the interests of the client and those of the opposing party. Whether the opposing party is likely to suffer prejudice depends on the nature of the case, the importance and probable tenor of the lawyer's testimony, and the probability that the lawyer's testimony will conflict with that of other witnesses. Even if there is risk of such prejudice, in determining whether the lawyer should be disqualified due regard must be given to the effect of disqualification on the lawyer's client. It is relevant that one or both parties could reasonably foresee that the lawyer would probably be a witness. The principle of imputed disqualification stated in Rule 1.10 has no application to this aspect of the problem.

Whether the combination of roles involves an improper conflict of interest with respect to the client is determined by Rule 1.7 or 1.9. For example, if there is likely to be substantial conflict between the testimony of the client and that of the lawyer or a member of the lawyer's firm, the representation is improper. The problem can arise whether the lawyer is called as a witness on behalf of the client or is called by the opposing party. Determining whether or not such a conflict exists is primarily the responsibility of the lawyer involved. See comment to Rule 1.7. If a lawyer who is a member of a firm may not act as both advocate and witness by reason of conflict of interest, Rule 1.10 disqualifies the firm also.

Rule: 3.8 Special Responsibilities of a Prosecutor

The prosecutor in a criminal case shall:
(a) refrain from prosecuting a charge that the prosecutor knows is not supported by probable cause;
(b) make reasonable efforts to assure that the accused has been advised of the right to, and the procedure for obtaining, counsel and has been given reasonable opportunity to obtain counsel;
(c) not seek to obtain from an unrepresented accused a waiver of important pretrial rights, such as the right to a preliminary hearing;
(d) make timely disclosure to the defense of all evidence or information known to the prosecutor that tends to negate the guilt of the accused or mitigates the degree of the offense, and, in connection with sentencing, disclose to the defense and to the tribunal all unprivileged mitigating information known to the prosecutor, except when the prosecutor is relieved of this responsibility by a protective order of the tribunal; and
(e) exercise reasonable care to prevent investigators, law enforcement personnel, employees, or other persons assisting or associated with the prosecutor in a criminal case from making an extrajudicial statement that the prosecutor would be prohibited from making under Rule 3.6.

Comment

A prosecutor has the responsibility of a minister of justice and not simply that of an advocate. This responsibility carries with it specific obligations to see that the defendant is accorded procedural justice and that guilt is decided upon the basis of sufficient evidence. Precisely how far the prosecutor is required to go in this direction is a matter of debate. Cf. Rule 3.3(d), governing ex parte proceedings, among which grand jury proceedings are included. Applicable law may require other measures by the prosecutor, and knowing disregard of those obligations or a systematic abuse of prosecutorial discretion could constitute a violation of Rule 8.4.

Paragraph (c) does not apply to an accused appearing pro se with the approval of the tribunal. Nor does it forbid the lawful questioning of a suspect who has knowingly waived the rights to counsel and silence.

The exception in paragraph (d) recognizes that a prosecutor may seek an appropriate protective order from the tribunal if disclosure of information to the defense could result in substantial harm to an individual or to the public interest.

In paragraphs (b) and (e), this rule imposes on a prosecutor an obligation to make reasonable efforts and to take reasonable care to assure that a defendant's rights are protected. Of course, not all of the individuals who might encroach upon those rights are under the control of the prosecutor. The prosecutor cannot be held responsible for the actions of persons over whom the prosecutor does not exercise authority. The prosecutor's obligation is discharged if the prosecutor has taken reasonable and appropriate steps to assure that the defendant's rights are protected.

Rule: 3.9 Advocate in Nonadjudicative Proceedings

A lawyer representing a client before a legislative or administrative tribunal in a nonadjudicative proceeding shall disclose that the appearance is in a representative capacity and shall conform to the provisions of Rules 3.3(a) through (c), 3.4(a) through (c), and 3.5.

Comment

In representation before bodies such as legislatures, municipal councils, and executive and administrative agencies acting in a rule-making or policy-making capacity, lawyers present facts, formulate issues, and advance argument in the matters under consideration. The decision-making body, like a court, should be able to rely on the integrity of the submissions made to it. A lawyer appearing before such a body should deal with the tribunal honestly and in conformity with applicable rules of procedure.

Lawyers have no exclusive right to appear before nonadjudicative bodies, as they do before a court. The requirements of this rule therefore may subject lawyers to regulations inapplicable to advocates who are not lawyers. However, legislatures and administrative agencies have a right to expect lawyers to deal with them as they deal with courts.

This rule does not apply to representation of a client in a negotiation or other bilateral transaction with a governmental agency; representation in such a transaction is governed by Rules 4.1 through 4.4.

Rules 4.1 - 4.4 Transactions with Persons Other Than Clients

Rule: 4.1 Truthfulness in Statements to Others

In the course of representing a client, a lawyer shall not knowingly make a false statement of material fact or law to a third person.

Comment

MISREPRESENTATION

A lawyer is required to be truthful when dealing with others on a client's behalf, but generally has no affirmative duty to inform an opposing party of relevant facts. A misrepresentation can occur if the lawyer incorporates or affirms a statement of another person that the lawyer knows is false.

STATEMENTS OF FACT

This rule refers to statements of fact. Whether a particular statement should be regarded as one of fact can depend on the circumstances. Under generally accepted conventions in negotiation, certain types of statements ordinarily are not taken as statements of material fact. Estimates of price or value placed on the subject of a transaction and a party's intentions as to an acceptable settlement of a claim are in this category, and so is the existence of an undisclosed principal except where nondisclosure of the principal would constitute fraud.

FRAUD BY CLIENT

Making a false statement may include the failure to make a statement in circumstances in which silence is equivalent to making such a statement. Thus, where the lawyer has made a statement that the lawyer believed to be true when made but later discovers that the statement was not true, in some circumstances failure to correct the statement may be equivalent to making a statement that is false. When the falsity of the original statement by the lawyer resulted from reliance upon what was told to the lawyer by the client and if the original statement if left uncorrected may further a criminal or fraudulent act by the client, the provisions of Rule 1.6(c)(3) give the lawyer discretion to make the disclosure necessary to rectify the consequences.

Rule: 4.2 Communication With a Person Represented by Counsel

In representing a client, a lawyer shall not communicate about the subject of the representation with a party whom the lawyer knows to be represented in the matter by another lawyer, unless the lawyer has the consent of the other lawyer or is authorized by law to do so.

Comment

This rule does not prohibit communication with a party, or an employee or agent of a party, concerning matters outside the representation. For example, the existence of a controversy between a government agency and a private party, or between two organizations, does not prohibit a lawyer for either from communicating with nonlawyer representatives of the other regarding a separate matter. Also, parties to a matter may communicate directly with each other and a lawyer having independent justification for communicating with the other party is permitted to do so. Communications authorized by law include, for example, the right of a party to a controversy with a government agency to speak with government officials about the matter.

In the case of an organization, this rule prohibits communications by a lawyer for one party concerning the matter in representation with persons having a managerial responsibility on behalf of the organization, and with any other person whose act or omission in connection with that matter may be imputed to the organization for purposes of civil or criminal liability or whose statement may constitute an admission on the part of the organization. If an agent or employee of the organization is represented in the matter by separate counsel, the consent by that counsel to a communication will be sufficient for purposes of this rule. Compare Rule 3.4(f).

This rule also covers any person, whether or not a party to a formal proceeding, who is represented by counsel concerning the matter in question.

Rule: 4.3 Dealing With an Unrepresented Person

In dealing on behalf of a client with a person who is not represented by counsel, a lawyer shall not state or imply that the lawyer is disinterested. When the lawyer knows or reasonably should know that the unrepresented person misunderstands the lawyer's role in the matter, the lawyer shall make reasonable efforts to correct the misunderstanding.

Comment

An unrepresented person, particularly one not experienced in dealing with legal matters, might assume that a lawyer is disinterested in loyalties or is a disinterested authority on the law even when the lawyer represents a client. During the course of a lawyer's representation of a client, the lawyer should not give advice to an unrepresented person other than the advice to obtain counsel.

Rule: 4.4 Respect for Rights of Third Persons

In representing a client, a lawyer shall not use means that have no substantial purpose other than to embarrass, delay, or burden a third person, or use methods of obtaining evidence that violate the legal rights of such a person.

Comment

Responsibility to a client requires a lawyer to subordinate the interests of others to those of the client, but that responsibility does not imply that a lawyer may disregard the rights of third persons. It is impractical to catalogue all such rights, but they include legal restrictions on methods of obtaining evidence from third persons.

Rules 5.1 - 5.6 Law Firms and Associations

Rule: 5.1 Responsibilities of a Partner or Supervisory Lawyer

(a) A partner in a law firm shall make reasonable efforts to ensure that the firm has in effect measures giving reasonable assurance that all lawyers in the firm conform to the Rules of Professional Conduct.

(b) A lawyer having direct supervisory authority over another lawyer shall make reasonable efforts to ensure that the other lawyer conforms to the Rules of Professional Conduct.

(c) A lawyer shall be responsible for another lawyer's violation of the rules of professional conduct if:

    (1) the lawyer orders or, with knowledge of the relevant facts and the specific conduct, ratifies the conduct involved; or

    (2) the lawyer is a partner in the law firm in which the other lawyer practices or has direct supervisory authority over the other lawyer, and knows of the conduct at a time when its consequences can be avoided or mitigated but fails to take reasonable remedial action.

Comment

Paragraphs (a) and (b) refer to lawyers who have supervisory authority over the professional work of a firm or a legal department of a government agency. This includes members of a partnership and the shareholders in a law firm organized as a professional corporation. This also includes lawyers having supervisory authority in the law department of an enterprise or government agency and lawyers who have intermediate managerial responsibilities in a firm.

The measures required to fulfill the responsibility prescribed in paragraphs (a) and (b) can depend on the firm's structure and the nature of its practice. In a small firm, informal supervision and occasional admonition ordinarily might be sufficient. In a large firm, or in practice situations in which intensely difficult ethical problems frequently arise, more elaborate procedures may be necessary. Some firms, for example, have a procedure whereby junior lawyers can make confidential referral of ethical problems directly to a designated senior partner or special committee. See Rule 5.2. Firms, whether large or small, may also rely on continuing legal education in professional ethics. In any event, the ethical atmosphere of a firm can influence the conduct of all its members and a lawyer having authority over the work of another may not assume that the subordinate lawyer will inevitably conform to the rules.

Paragraph (c)(1) expresses a general principle concerning responsibility for acts of another. See also Rule 8.4(a).

Paragraph (c)(2) defines the duty of a lawyer having direct supervisory authority over performance of specific legal work by another lawyer. Whether a lawyer has such supervisory authority in particular circumstances is a question of fact. Partners of a private firm have at least indirect responsibility for all work being done by the firm, while a partner in charge of a particular matter ordinarily has direct authority over other firm lawyers engaged in the matter. Appropriate remedial action by a partner would depend on the immediacy of the partner's involvement and the seriousness of the misconduct. The supervisor is required to intervene to prevent avoidable consequences of misconduct if the supervisor knows that the misconduct occurred. Thus, if a supervising lawyer knows that a subordinate misrepresented a matter to an opposing party in negotiation, the supervisor as well as the subordinate has a duty to correct the resulting misapprehension.

Professional misconduct by a lawyer under supervision could reveal a violation of paragraph (b) on the part of the supervisory lawyer even though it does not entail a violation of paragraph (c) because there was no direction, ratification, or knowledge of the violation.

Apart from this rule and Rule 8.4(a), a lawyer does not have disciplinary liability for the conduct of a partner, associate, or subordinate. Whether a lawyer may be liable civilly or criminally for another lawyer's conduct is a question of law beyond the scope of these rules.

Rule: 5.2 Responsibilities of a Subordinate Lawyer

(a) A lawyer is bound by the rules of professional conduct notwithstanding that the lawyer acted at the direction of another person.

(b) A subordinate lawyer does not violate the rules of professional conduct if that lawyer acts in accordance with a supervisory lawyer's reasonable resolution of an arguable question of professional duty.

Comment

Although a lawyer is not relieved of responsibility for a violation by the fact that the lawyer acted at the direction of a supervisor, that fact may be relevant in determining whether a lawyer had the knowledge required to render conduct a violation of the rules. For example, if a subordinate filed a frivolous pleading at the direction of a supervisor, the subordinate would not be guilty of a professional violation unless the subordinate knew of the document's frivolous character.

When lawyers in a supervisor-subordinate relationship encounter a matter involving professional judgment as to ethical duty, the supervisor may assume responsibility for making the judgment. Otherwise a consistent course of action or position could not be taken. If the question can reasonably be answered only one way, the duty of both lawyers is clear and they are equally responsible for fulfilling it. However, if the question is reasonably arguable, someone has to decide upon the course of action. That authority ordinarily reposes in the supervisor, and a subordinate may be guided accordingly. For example, if a question arises whether the interests of two clients conflict under Rule 1.7, the supervisor's reasonable resolution of the question should protect the subordinate professionally if the resolution is subsequently challenged.

Rule: 5.3 Responsibilities Regarding Nonlawyer Assistants

With respect to a nonlawyer employed by, retained by, or associated with a lawyer:

(a) a partner in a law firm shall make reasonable efforts to ensure that the firm has in effect measures giving reasonable assurance that the person's conduct is compatible with the professional obligations of the lawyer;

(b) a lawyer having direct supervisory authority over the nonlawyer shall make reasonable efforts to ensure that the person's conduct is compatible with the professional obligations of the lawyer; and

(c) a lawyer shall be responsible for conduct of such a person that would be a violation of the rules of professional conduct if engaged in by a lawyer if:

(1) the lawyer orders or, with knowledge of the relevant facts and the specific conduct, ratifies the conduct involved; or

(2) the lawyer is a partner in the law firm in which the person is employed or has direct supervisory authority over the person and knows of the conduct at a time when its consequences can be avoided or mitigated but fails to take reasonable remedial action.

Comment

Lawyers generally employ assistants in their practice, including secretaries, investigators, law student interns, and paraprofessionals. Such assistants, whether employees or independent contractors, act for the lawyer in rendition of the lawyer's professional services. A lawyer should give such assistants appropriate instruction and supervision concerning the ethical aspects of their employment, particularly regarding the obligation not to disclose information relating to representation of the client, and should be responsible for their work product. The measures employed in supervising nonlawyers should take account of the fact that they do not have legal training and are not subject to professional discipline.

As does Rule 3.8, this rule may in certain situations impose on a prosecutor an obligation to make reasonable efforts to assure that a defendant's rights are protected. Of course, not all of the individuals who might encroach upon those rights are under the control of the prosecutor, but where this rule applies, the prosecutor must take reasonable and appropriate steps to assure that the defendant's rights are protected.

Rule: 5.4 Professional Independence of a Lawyer

(a) A lawyer or law firm shall not share legal fees with a nonlawyer, except that:

(1) an agreement by a lawyer with the lawyer's firm, partner, or associate may provide for the payment of money, over a reasonable period of time after the lawyer's death, to the lawyer's estate, or to one or more specified persons;

(2) a lawyer who purchases the practice of a deceased, disabled, or disappeared lawyer may, pursuant to the provisions of Rule 1.17, pay to the estate or other representative of that lawyer the agreed-upon purchase price;

(3) a lawyer or law firm may include nonlawyer employees in a compensation or retirement plan, even though the plan is based in whole or in part on a profit-sharing arrangement; and

(4)   a lawyer may share court-awarded legal fees with a nonprofit organization that employed, retained, or recommended employment of the lawyer in the matter.

(b)   A lawyer shall not form a partnership with a nonlawyer if any of the activities of the partnership consist of the practice of law.

(c)   A lawyer shall not permit a person who recommends, employs, or pays the lawyer to render legal services for another to direct or regulate the lawyer's professional judgment in rendering such legal services.

(d)   A lawyer shall not practice with or in the form of a professional corporation or association authorized to practice law for a profit, if:

(1)   a nonlawyer owns any interest therein, except that a fiduciary representative of the estate of a lawyer may hold the stock or interest of the lawyer for a reasonable time during administration;

(2)   a nonlawyer is a corporate director or officer thereof, or one who occupies a position of similar responsibility in any form of association other than a coporation; or

(3)   a nonlawyer has the right to direct or control the professional judgment of a lawyer.

Comment

The provisions of this rule express traditional limitations on sharing fees. These limitations are to protect the lawyer's professional independence of judgment. Where someone other than the client pays the lawyer's fee or salary, or recommends employment of the lawyer, that arrangement does not modify the lawyer's obligation to the client. As stated in paragraph (c), such arrangements should not interfere with the lawyer's professional judgment.

This rule also expresses traditional limitations on permitting a third party to direct or regulate the lawyer's professional judgment in rendering legal services to another. See also Rule 1.8(f) (lawyer may accept compensation from a third party as long as there is no interference with the lawyer's independent professional judgment and the client gives consent.

Rule: 5.5 Unauthorized Practice of Law; Multijurisdictional Practice of Law

(a)   A lawyer shall not practice law in a jurisdiction in violation of the regulation of the legal profession in that jurisdiction, or assist another in doing so.

(b)   A lawyer who is not admitted to practice in this jurisdiction shall not:

(1)   except as authorized by law or these rules, establish an office or other systematic and continuous presence in this jurisdiction for the practice of law; or

(2) hold out to the public or otherwise represent that the lawyer is admitted to practice law in this jurisdiction.

(c) A lawyer admitted in another jurisdiction of the United States and not disbarred or suspended from practice in any jurisdiction may provide temporary legal services in this jurisdiction that:

(1) are undertaken in association with a lawyer who is admitted to practice in this jurisdiction and who actively participates in the matter;

(2) are in or reasonably related to a pending or potential proceeding before a tribunal in this or another jurisdiction, if the lawyer or a person the lawyer is assisting is authorized by law to appear in such proceeding or reasonably expects to be so authorized;

(3) are in or reasonably related to a pending or potential arbitration, mediation, or other alternative dispute resolution proceeding in this or another jurisdiction, if the services arise out of or are reasonably related to the lawyer's practice in a jurisdiction in which the lawyer is admitted to practice and are not services for which the forum requires pro hac vice admission; or

(4) are not covered by paragraphs (c)(2) or (c)(3) and arise out of or are reasonably related to the lawyer's practice in a jurisdiction in which the lawyer is admitted to practice.

(d) A lawyer admitted in another jurisdiction of the United States and not disbarred or suspended from practice in any jurisdiction may provide legal services in this jurisdiction that:

(1) are provided to the lawyer's employer or its organizational affiliates and are not services for which the forum requires pro hac vice admission; or

(2) are services that the lawyer is authorized by law to provide in this jurisdiction.

Comment

A lawyer may practice law only in a jurisdiction in which the lawyer is authorized to practice. A lawyer may be admitted to practice law in a jurisdiction on a regular basis or may be authorized by law, order, or court rule to practice for a limited purpose or on a restricted basis. See, for example, MCR 8.126, which permits, under certain circumstances, the temporary admission to the bar of a person who is licensed to practice law in another jurisdiction, and Rule 5(E) of the Rules for the Board of Law Examiners, which permits a lawyer who is admitted to practice in a foreign country to practice in Michigan as a special legal consultant, without examination, provided certain conditions are met. Paragraph (a) applies to the unauthorized practice of law by a lawyer, whether through the lawyer's direct action or by the lawyer assisting another person. The definition of the practice of law is established by law and varies from one jurisdiction to another. Whatever the definition, limiting the practice of law to members of the bar protects the public against rendition of legal services by unqualified persons. This rule does not prohibit a lawyer from employing the services of paraprofessionals and delegating functions to them, so long as the lawyer supervises the delegated work and retains responsibility for it. See Rule 5.3. A lawyer may provide professional advice and instruction to nonlawyers whose employment requires knowledge of the law, for example, claims adjusters, employees of financial or commercial institutions, social workers, accountants and persons employed in government agencies. Lawyers also may assist independent nonlawyers, such as paraprofessionals, who are authorized by the law of a jurisdiction to provide particular law-related services. In addition, a lawyer may counsel nonlawyers who wish to proceed pro se.

Other than as authorized by law or this rule, a lawyer who is not admitted to practice generally in this jurisdiction violates paragraph (b) if the lawyer establishes an office or other systematic and continuous presence in this jurisdiction for the practice of law. Presence may be systematic and continuous even if the lawyer is not physically present here. Such a lawyer must not hold out to the public or otherwise represent that the lawyer is admitted to practice law in this jurisdiction. See also Rules 7.1(a) and 7.5(b).

There are occasions on which a lawyer admitted to practice in another jurisdiction of the United States and not disbarred or suspended from practice in any jurisdiction may provide legal services on a temporary basis in this jurisdiction under circumstances that do not create an unreasonable risk to the interests of clients, the public, or the courts. Paragraph (c) identifies four such circumstances. The fact that conduct is not so identified does not indicate whether the conduct is authorized. With the exception of paragraphs (d)(1) and (d)(2), this rule does not authorize a lawyer to establish an office or other systematic and continuous presence in this jurisdiction without being admitted here to practice generally.

There is no single test to determine whether a lawyer's services are provided on a "temporary basis" in this jurisdiction and, therefore, may be permissible under paragraph (c). Services may be "temporary" even though the lawyer provides services in this jurisdiction on a recurring basis or for an extended period of time, as when the lawyer is representing a client in a single lengthy negotiation or litigation.

Paragraphs (c) and (d) apply to lawyers who are admitted to practice law in any jurisdiction of the United States, including the District of Columbia and any state, territory, or commonwealth. The word "admitted" in paragraph (c) contemplates that the lawyer is authorized to practice and is in good standing to practice in the jurisdiction in which the lawyer is admitted and excludes a lawyer who, while technically admitted, is not authorized to practice because, for example, the lawyer is on inactive status or is suspended for nonpayment of dues.

Paragraph (c)(1) recognizes that the interests of clients and the public are protected if a lawyer admitted only in another jurisdiction associates with a lawyer licensed to practice in this jurisdiction. For this paragraph to apply, however, the lawyer admitted to practice in this jurisdiction must actively participate in and share responsibility for the representation of the client.

Lawyers not admitted to practice generally in a jurisdiction may be authorized by law or order of a tribunal or an administrative agency to appear before the tribunal or agency. This authority may be granted pursuant to formal rules governing admission pro hac vice, such as MCR 8.126, or pursuant to informal practice of the tribunal or agency. Under paragraph (c)(2), a lawyer does not violate this rule when the lawyer appears before a tribunal or agency pursuant to such authority. To the extent that a law or court rule of this jurisdiction requires that a lawyer who is not admitted to practice in this jurisdiction obtain admission pro hac vice before appearing before a tribunal or administrative agency, this rule requires the lawyer to obtain that authority.

Paragraph (c)(2) also provides that a lawyer rendering services in this jurisdiction on a temporary basis does not violate this rule when the lawyer engages in conduct in anticipation of a proceeding or hearing in a jurisdiction in which the lawyer is authorized to practice law or in which the lawyer reasonably expects to be admitted pro hac vice under MCR 8.126. Examples of such conduct include meetings with a client, interviews of potential witnesses, and the review of documents. Similarly, a lawyer admitted only in another jurisdiction may engage temporarily in this jurisdiction in conduct related to pending litigation in another jurisdiction in which the lawyer is or reasonably expects to be authorized to appear, including taking depositions in this jurisdiction.

When a lawyer has been or reasonably expects to be admitted to appear before a court or administrative agency, paragraph (c)(2) also permits conduct by lawyers who are associated with that lawyer in the matter but who do not expect to appear before the court or administrative agency. For example, subordinate lawyers may conduct research, review documents, and attend meetings with witnesses in support of the lawyer responsible for the litigation.

Paragraph (c)(3) permits a lawyer admitted to practice law in another jurisdiction to perform services on a temporary basis in this jurisdiction, provided that those services are in or are reasonably related to a pending or potential arbitration, mediation, or other alternative dispute resolution proceeding in this or another jurisdiction and the services arise out of or are reasonably related to the lawyer's practice in a jurisdiction in which the lawyer is admitted to practice. The lawyer, however, must obtain admission pro hac vice under MCR 8.126 in the case of a court-annexed arbitration or mediation, or otherwise if required by court rule or law.

Paragraph (c)(4) permits a lawyer admitted in another jurisdiction to provide certain legal services on a temporary basis in this jurisdiction if they arise out of or are reasonably related to the lawyer's practice in a jurisdiction in which the lawyer is admitted but are not covered by paragraphs (c)(2) or (c)(3). These services include both legal services and services performed by nonlawyers that would be considered the practice of law if performed by lawyers.

Paragraphs (c)(3) and (c)(4) require that the services arise out of or be reasonably related to the lawyer's practice in a jurisdiction in which the lawyer is admitted. A variety of factors indicate such a relationship. The lawyer's client previously may have been represented by the lawyer or may reside in or have substantial contacts with the jurisdiction in which the lawyer is admitted. The matter, although involving other jurisdictions, may have a significant connection with that jurisdiction. In other cases, significant aspects of the lawyer's work may be conducted in that jurisdiction or a significant aspect of the matter may involve the law of that jurisdiction. The necessary relationship may arise when the client's activities or the legal issues involve multiple jurisdictions, such as when the officers of a multinational corporation survey potential business sites and seek the services of the corporation's lawyer in assessing the relative merits of each. In addition, the services may draw on the lawyer's recognized expertise, as developed through the regular practice of law on behalf of clients in matters involving a particular body of federal, nationally uniform, foreign, or international law.

Paragraph (d) identifies two circumstances in which a lawyer who is admitted to practice in another jurisdiction of the United States and is not disbarred or suspended from practice in any jurisdiction may establish an office or other systematic and continuous presence in this jurisdiction for the practice of law as well as to provide legal services on a temporary basis. Except as provided in paragraphs (d)(1) and (d)(2), a lawyer who is admitted to practice law in another jurisdiction and who establishes an office or other systematic or continuous presence in this jurisdiction must become admitted to practice law generally in this jurisdiction.

Paragraph (d)(1) applies to a lawyer who is employed by a client to provide legal services to the client or its organizational affiliates, i.e., entities that control, are controlled by, or are under common control with the employer. This paragraph does not authorize the provision of personal legal services to the employer's officers or employees. This paragraph applies to in-house corporate lawyers, government lawyers, and others who are employed to render legal services to the employer. The lawyer's ability to represent the employer outside the jurisdiction in which the lawyer is licensed generally serves the interests of the employer and does not create an unreasonable risk to the client and others because the employer is well situated to assess the lawyer's qualifications and the quality of the lawyer's work.

If an employed lawyer establishes an office or other systematic presence in this jurisdiction for the purpose of rendering legal services to the employer, the lawyer may be subject to registration or other requirements, including assessments for client protection funds and mandatory continuing legal education.

Paragraph (d)(2) recognizes that a lawyer may provide legal services in a jurisdiction in which the lawyer is not licensed when authorized to do so by statute, court rule, executive regulation, or judicial precedent.

A lawyer who practices law in this jurisdiction is subject to the disciplinary authority of this jurisdiction. See Rule 8.5(a).

In some circumstances, a lawyer who practices law in this jurisdiction pursuant to paragraphs (c) or (d) may be required to inform the client that the lawyer is not licensed to practice law in this jurisdiction. For example, such disclosure may be required when the representation occurs primarily in this jurisdiction and requires knowledge of the law of this jurisdiction. See Rule 1.4(b).

Paragraphs (c) and (d) do not authorize lawyers who are admitted to practice in other jurisdictions to advertise legal services to prospective clients in this jurisdiction. Whether and how lawyers may communicate the availability of their services to prospective clients in this jurisdiction is governed by Rules 7.1 to 7.5.

Rule: 5.6 Restrictions on Right to Practice

A lawyer shall not participate in offering or making:
(a) a partnership or employment agreement that restricts the right of a lawyer to practice after termination of the relationship, except an agreement concerning benefits upon retirement or as permitted in Rule 1.17; or
(b) an agreement in which a restriction on the lawyer's right to practice is part of the settlement of a controversy between private parties.

Comment

An agreement restricting the right of a lawyer to practice after leaving a firm not only limits the lawyer's professional autonomy but also limits the freedom of clients to choose a lawyer. Paragraph (a) prohibits such agreements except for restrictions incident to provisions concerning retirement benefits for service with the firm or restrictions included in the terms of a sale pursuant to MRPC 1.17.

Paragraph (b) prohibits a lawyer from agreeing not to represent other persons in connection with settling a claim on behalf of a client.

Rule 5.7 Responsibilities Regarding Law-Related Services

(a) A lawyer shall be subject to the Michigan Rules of Professional Conduct with respect to the provision of law-related services, as defined in paragraph (b), if the law-related services are provided:

    (1) by the lawyer in circumstances that are not distinct from the lawyer's provision of legal services to clients; or

    (2) in other circumstances by an entity controlled by the lawyer individually or with others if the lawyer fails to take reasonable measures to assure that a person obtaining the law-related services knows that the services are not legal services and that the protections of the client-lawyer relationship do not exist.

(b) The term "law-related services" denotes services that might reasonably be performed in conjunction with and in substance are related to the provision of legal services, and that are not prohibited as unauthorized practice of law when provided by a nonlawyer.

Comment

When a lawyer performs law-related services or controls an organization that does so, there exists the potential for ethical problems. Principal among these is the possibility that the person for whom the law-related services are performed fails to understand that the services may not carry with them the protections normally afforded as part of the client-lawyer relationship. The recipient of the law-related services may expect, for example, that the protection of client confidences, prohibitions against representation of persons with conflicting interests, and obligations of a lawyer to maintain professional independence apply to the provision of law-related services when that may not be the case.

Rule 5.7 applies to the provision of law-related services by a lawyer even when the lawyer does not provide any legal services to the person for whom the law-related services are performed, and regardless of whether the law-related services are performed through a law firm or a separate entity. This rule identifies the circumstances in which all the Michigan Rules of Professional Conduct apply to the provision of law-related services. Even when those circumstances do not exist, however, the conduct of a lawyer involved in the provision of law-related services is subject to those rules that apply generally to lawyer conduct, regardless whether the conduct involves the provision of legal services. See, e.g., Rule 8.4.

When law-related services are provided by a lawyer under circumstances that are not distinct from the lawyer's provision of legal services to clients, the lawyer providing the law-related services must adhere to the requirements of the Michigan Rules of Professional Conduct as provided in paragraph (a)(1). Even when the law-related and legal services are provided in circumstances that are distinct from each other, for example through separate entities or different support staff within the law firm, the Michigan Rules of Professional Conduct apply to the lawyer as provided in paragraph (a)(2) unless the lawyer takes reasonable measures to assure that the recipient of the law-related services knows that the services are not legal services and that the protections of the client-lawyer relationship do not apply.

Law-related services also may be provided through an entity that is distinct from that through which the lawyer provides legal services. If the lawyer individually or with others has control of such an entity's operations, this rule requires the lawyer to take reasonable measures to assure that each person using the services of the entity knows that the services provided by the entity are not legal services and that the Michigan Rules of Professional Conduct that relate to the client-lawyer relationship do not apply. A lawyer's control of an entity extends to the ability to direct its operation. Whether a lawyer has such control will depend upon the circumstances of the particular case.

When a client-lawyer relationship exists with a person who is referred by a lawyer to a separate law-related service entity controlled by the lawyer, individually or with others, the lawyer must comply with Rule 1.8(a).

In taking the reasonable measures referred to in paragraph (a)(2) to assure that a person using law-related services understands the practical effect or significance of the inapplicability of the Michigan Rules of Professional Conduct, the lawyer should communicate to the person receiving the law-related services, in a manner sufficient to assure that the person understands the significance of the fact, that the relationship of the person to the business entity will not be a client-lawyer relationship. The communication should be made, preferably in writing, before law-related services are provided or before an agreement is reached for provision of such services.

The burden is upon the lawyer to show that the lawyer has taken reasonable measures under the circumstances to communicate the desired understanding. For instance, a sophisticated user of law-related services, such as a publicly held corporation, may require a lesser explanation than someone unaccustomed to making distinctions between legal services and law-related services, such as an individual seeking tax advice from a lawyer-accountant or investigative services in connection with a lawsuit.

Regardless of the sophistication of potential recipients of law-related services, a lawyer should take special care to keep separate the provision of law-related and legal services in order to minimize the risk that the recipient will assume that the law-related services are legal services. The risk of such confusion is especially acute when the lawyer renders both types of services with respect to the same matter. Under some circumstances, the legal and law-related services may be so closely entwined that they cannot be distinguished from each other, and the requirement of disclosure and consultation imposed by paragraph (a)(2) of the rule cannot be met. In such a case, a lawyer will be responsible for assuring that both the lawyer's conduct and, to the extent required by Rule 5.3, that of nonlawyer employees in the distinct entity that the lawyer controls, comply in all respects with the Michigan Rules of Professional Conduct.

A broad range of economic and other interests of clients may be served by lawyers' engaging in the delivery of law-related services. Examples of law-related services include providing title insurance, financial planning, accounting, trust services, real estate counseling, legislative lobbying, economic analysis, social work, psychological counseling, tax preparation, and patent, medical, or environmental consulting.

When a lawyer is obliged to accord the recipients of such services the protections of those rules that apply to the client-lawyer relationship, the lawyer must take special care to heed the proscriptions of the rules addressing conflicts of interest, and to scrupulously adhere to the requirements of Rule 1.6 relating to disclosure of confidential information. The promotion of the law-related services must also in all respects comply with Rules 7.1 through 7.3, dealing with advertising and solicitation. In that regard, lawyers should take special care to identify the obligations that may be imposed as a result of a jurisdiction's decisional law.

When the full protections of all the Michigan Rules of Professional Conduct do not apply to the provision of law-related services, principles of law external to the rules, for example, the law of principal and agent, govern the legal duties owed to those receiving the services. Those other legal principles may establish a different degree of protection for the recipient with respect to confidentiality of information, conflicts of interest, and permissible business relationships with clients. See also Rule 8.4 (Misconduct).

Rules 6.1 - 6.6 Public Service

Rule: 6.1 Pro Bono Publico Service

A lawyer should render public interest legal service. A lawyer may discharge this responsibility by providing professional services at no fee or a reduced fee to persons of limited means, or to public service or charitable groups or organizations.

A lawyer may also discharge this responsibility by service in activities for improving the law, the legal system, or the legal profession, and by financial support for organizations that provide legal services to persons of limited means.

Comment

The ABA House of Delegates has formally acknowledged "the basic responsibility of each lawyer engaged in the practice of law to provide public interest legal services" without fee, or at a substantially reduced fee, in one or more of the following areas: poverty law, civil rights law, public rights law, charitable organization representation and the administration of justice. This rule expresses that policy, but is not intended to be enforced through disciplinary process.

The rights and responsibilities of individuals and organizations in the United States are increasingly defined in legal terms. As a consequence, legal assistance in coping with the web of statutes, rules and regulations is imperative for persons of modest and limited means, as well as for the relatively well-to-do.

The basic responsibility for providing legal services for those unable to pay ultimately rests upon the individual lawyer, and personal involvement in the problems of the disadvantaged can be one of the most rewarding experiences in the life of a lawyer. Every lawyer, regardless of professional prominence or professional workload, should find time to participate in or otherwise support the provision of legal services to the disadvantaged. The provision of free legal services to those unable to pay reasonable fees continues to be an obligation of each lawyer as well as the profession generally, but the efforts of individual lawyers are often not enough to meet the need. Thus, it has been necessary for the profession and government to institute additional programs to provide legal services. Accordingly, legal aid offices, lawyer referral services and other related programs have been developed, and others will be developed by the profession and government. Every lawyer should support all proper efforts to meet this need for legal services.

Rule: 6.2 Accepting Appointments

A lawyer shall not seek to avoid appointment by a tribunal to represent a person except for good cause, such as:
(a) representing the client is likely to result in violation of the Rules of Professional Conduct or other law;
(b) representing the client is likely to result in an unreasonable financial burden on the lawyer; or
(c) the client or the cause is so repugnant to the lawyer as to be likely to impair the client-lawyer relationship or the lawyer's ability to represent the client.

Comment

A lawyer ordinarily is not obliged to accept a client whose character or cause the lawyer regards as repugnant. The lawyer's freedom to select clients is, however, qualified. All lawyers have a responsibility to assist in providing pro bono publico service. See Rule 6.1. An individual lawyer fulfills this responsibility by accepting a fair share of unpopular matters or indigent or unpopular clients. A lawyer may also be subject to appointment by a court to serve unpopular clients or persons unable to afford legal services.

APPOINTED COUNSEL

For good cause, a lawyer may seek to decline an appointment to represent a person who cannot afford to retain counsel or whose cause is unpopular. Good cause exists if the lawyer could not handle the matter competently (see Rule 1.1) or if undertaking the representation would result in an improper conflict of interest. Good cause also exists if the client or the cause is so repugnant to the lawyer as to be likely to impair the client-lawyer relationship or the lawyer's ability to represent the client. A lawyer may also seek to decline an appointment if acceptance would be unreasonably burdensome, for example, when it would impose a financial sacrifice so great as to be unjust.

An appointed lawyer has the same obligations to the client as retained counsel, including the obligations of loyalty and confidentiality, and is subject to the same limitations on the client-lawyer relationship, such as the obligation to refrain from assisting the client in violation of the rules.

Rule: 6.3 Legal Services Organizations and Lawyer Referral Services

(a) A lawyer may serve as a director, officer, or member of a legal services organization, apart from the law firm in which the lawyer practices, notwithstanding that the organization serves persons having interests adverse to a client of the lawyer. The lawyer shall not knowingly participate in a decision or action of the organization:

   (1) if participating in the decision or action would be incompatible with the lawyer's obligations to a client under Rule 1.7; or

   (2) where the decision or action could have a material adverse effect on the representation of a client of the organization whose interests are adverse to a client of the lawyer.

(b) A lawyer may participate in and pay the usual charges of a not-for-profit lawyer referral service that recommends legal services to the public if that service:

   (1) maintains registration as a qualified service with the State Bar, under such rules as may be adopted by the State Bar, consistent with these rules;

   (2) is operated in the public interest for the purpose of referring prospective clients to lawyers; pro bono and public service legal programs; and government, consumer or other agencies that can best

provide the assistance needed by clients, in light of their financial circumstances, spoken language, any disability, geographical convenience, and the nature and complexity of their problems;

(3) is open to all lawyers licensed and eligible to practice in this state who maintain an office within the geographical area served, and who:

    (i) meet reasonable and objective requirements of experience, as established by the service;

    (ii) pay reasonable registration and membership fees not to exceed an amount established by the State Bar to encourage widespread lawyer participation; and

    (iii) maintain a policy of errors and omissions insurance, or provide proof of financial responsibility, in an amount at least equal to the minimum established by the State Bar;

(4) ensures that the combined fees and expenses charged a prospective client by a qualified service and a lawyer to whom the client is referred not exceed the total charges the client would have incurred had no referral service been involved; and

(5) makes no fee-generating referral to any lawyer who has an ownership interest in, or who operates or is employed by, the qualified service, or who is associated with a law firm that has an ownership interest in, or operates or is employed by, a qualified service.

(c) The requirements of subrule (b) do not apply to

(1) a plan of prepaid legal services insurance authorized to operate in the state, or a group or prepaid legal plan, whether operated by a union, trust, mutual benefit or aid association, corporation or other entity or person, which provides unlimited or a specified amount of telephone advice or personal communications at no charge to the members or beneficiaries, other than a periodic membership or beneficiary fee, and furnishes to or pays for legal services for its members or beneficiaries;

(2) individual lawyer-to-lawyer referrals;

(3) lawyers jointly advertising their services in a manner that discloses that such advertising is solely to solicit clients for themselves; or

(4) any pro bono legal assistance program that does not accept fees from lawyers or clients for referrals.

(d) The State Bar or any aggrieved person may seek an injunction in the circuit court to enjoin violations of subrule (b). In the event the injunction is granted, the petitioner shall be entitled to reasonable costs and attorney fees.

(e) A lawyer may participate in and pay the usual charges of a plan or organization defined in subrule (c)(1), if that plan or organization:

(1) has filed with the State Bar of Michigan a written plan disclosing the name under which it operates; the name, address, and telephone number of its chief operating officer; and the plan terms, conditions

of eligibility, schedule of benefits, subscription charges and agreements with counsel;

(2) updates its filings within 30 days of any material change;

(3) in January of each year following its inception files a statement representing that it continues to do business under the terms and conditions reflected in its filings as amended to date.

These filing requirements shall not apply to not-for-profit legal aid associations.

Comment

Lawyers should be encouraged to support and participate in legal service organizations. A lawyer who is an officer or a member of such an organization does not thereby have a client-lawyer relationship with persons served by the organization. However, there is potential conflict between the interests of such persons and the interests of the lawyer's clients. If the possibility of such conflict disqualified a lawyer from serving on the board of a legal services organization, the profession's involvement in such organizations would be severely curtailed.

It may be necessary in appropriate cases to reassure a client of the organization that the representation will not be affected by conflicting loyalties of a member of the board. Established, written policies in this respect can enhance the credibility of such assurances.

The restriction on lawyer participation with legal services and lawyer referral service organizations to those that file their plans with the State Bar of Michigan is intended to facilitate the establishment of a single, central repository of all such organizations in Michigan and of the terms and conditions under which they operate. The existence of that repository would make it possible for the State Bar of Michigan annually to prepare and make publicly available a directory of legal services and lawyer referral service organizations in Michigan. Absent such a central repository, reliable information concerning the status of all such organizations might not be available.

The 1990 amendment to MRPC 6.3(b) was made at the request of the State Bar of Michigan.

Rule: 6.4 Law Reform Activities Affecting Client Interests

A lawyer may serve as a director, officer, or member of an organization involved in reform of the law or administration of the law notwithstanding that the reform may affect the interests of a client of the lawyer. When the lawyer knows that the interests of a client may be materially benefitted by a decision in which the lawyer participates, the lawyer shall disclose that fact but need not identify the client.

Lawyers involved in organizations seeking law reform generally do not have a client-lawyer relationship with the organization. Otherwise, it might follow that a lawyer could not be involved in a bar association law reform program that might indirectly affect a client. See also the comment to Rule 1.2. For example, a lawyer specializing in antitrust litigation might be regarded as disqualified from participating in drafting revisions of rules governing that subject. In determining the nature and scope of participation in such activities, a lawyer should be mindful of obligations to clients under other rules, particularly Rule 1.7. A lawyer is professionally obligated to protect the integrity of the program by making an appropriate disclosure within the organization when the lawyer knows a private client might be materially benefitted.

Rule: 6.5 Professional Conduct

(a) A lawyer shall treat with courtesy and respect all persons involved in the legal process. A lawyer shall take particular care to avoid treating such a person discourteously or disrespectfully because of the person's race, gender, or other protected personal characteristic. To the extent possible, a lawyer shall require subordinate lawyers and nonlawyer assistants to provide such courteous and respectful treatment.

(b) A lawyer serving as an adjudicative officer shall, without regard to a person's race, gender, or other protected personal characteristic, treat every person fairly, with courtesy and respect. To the extent possible, the lawyer shall require staff and others who are subject to the adjudicative officer's direction and control to provide such fair, courteous, and respectful treatment to persons who have contact with the adjudicative tribunal.

Comment

DUTIES OF THE LAWYER

A lawyer is an officer of the court who has sworn to uphold the federal and state constitutions, to proceed only by means that are truthful and honorable, and to avoid offensive personality. It follows that such a professional must treat clients and third persons with courtesy and respect. For many citizens, contact with a lawyer is the first or only contact with the legal system. Respect for law and for legal institutions is diminished whenever a lawyer neglects the obligation to treat persons properly. It is increased when the obligation is met.

A lawyer must pursue a client's interests with diligence. This often requires the lawyer to frame questions and statements in bold and direct terms. The obligation to treat persons with courtesy and respect is not inconsistent with the lawyer's right, where appropriate, to speak and write bluntly. Obviously, it is not possible to formulate a rule that will clearly divide what is properly challenging from what is impermissibly rude. A lawyer's professional judgment must be employed here with care and discretion.

A lawyer must take particular care to avoid words or actions that appear to be improperly based upon a person's race, gender, or other protected personal characteristic. Legal institutions, and those who serve them, should take leadership roles in assuring equal treatment for all.

A judge must act "[a]t all times" in a manner that promotes public confidence in the impartiality of the judiciary. Canon 2(B) of the Code of Judicial Conduct. See also Canon 5. By contrast, a lawyer's private conduct is largely beyond the scope of these rules. See Rule 8.4. However, a lawyer's private conduct should not cast doubt on the lawyer's commitment to equal justice under law.

A supervisory lawyer should make every reasonable effort to ensure that subordinate lawyers and nonlawyer assistants, as well as other agents, avoid discourteous or disrespectful behavior toward persons involved in the legal process. Further, a supervisory lawyer should make reasonable efforts to ensure that the firm has in effect policies and procedures that do not discriminate against members or employees of the firm on the basis of race, gender, or other protected personal characteristic. See Rules 5.1 and 5.3.

DUTIES OF ADJUDICATIVE OFFICERS

The duties of an adjudicative officer are included in these rules, since many legislatively created adjudicative positions, such as administrative hearing officer, are not covered by the Code of Judicial Conduct. For parallel provisions for judges, see the Code of Judicial Conduct.

Rule 6.6 Nonprofit and Court-Annexed Limited Legal Services Programs

(a) A lawyer who, under the auspices of a program sponsored by a nonprofit organization or court, provides short-term limited legal services to a client without expectation by either the lawyer or the client that the lawyer will provide continuing representation in the matter:

    (1) is subject to Rules 1.7 and 1.9(a) only if the lawyer knows that the representation of the client involves a conflict of interest; and

(2) is subject to Rule 1.10 only if the lawyer knows that another lawyer associated with the lawyer in a law firm is disqualified by Rule 1.7 or 1.9(a) with respect to the matter.

(b) Except as provided in paragraph (a)(2), Rule 1.10 is inapplicable to a representation governed by this rule.

Comment

Legal services organizations, courts, and various nonprofit organizations have established programs through which lawyers provide short-term limited legal services, such as advice or the completion of legal forms, that will help persons address their legal problems without further representation by a lawyer. In these programs, such as legal-advice hotlines, advice-only clinics, or pro se counseling programs, a client-lawyer relationship may or may not be established as a matter of law, but regardless there is no expectation that the lawyer's representation of the client will continue beyond the limited consultation. Such programs are normally operated under circumstances in which it is not feasible for a lawyer to systematically screen for conflicts of interest as is generally required before undertaking a representation. See, e.g., Rules 1.7, 1.9, and 1.10.

A lawyer who provides short-term limited legal services pursuant to this rule must secure the client's consent to the scope of the representation. See Rule 1.2. If a short-term limited representation would not be reasonable under the circumstances, the lawyer may offer advice to the client but must also advise the client of the need for further assistance of counsel. Except as provided in this rule, the Michigan Rules of Professional Conduct, including Rules 1.6 and 1.9(c), are applicable to the limited representation.

Because a lawyer who is representing a client in the circumstances addressed by this rule ordinarily is not able to check systematically for conflicts of interest, paragraph (a) requires compliance with Rules 1.7 or 1.9(a) only if the lawyer knows that the representation presents a conflict of interest for the lawyer, and with Rule 1.10 only if the lawyer knows that another lawyer in the lawyer's firm is disqualified by Rules 1.7 or 1.9(a) in the matter.

Because the limited nature of the services significantly reduces the risk of conflicts of interest with other matters being handled by the lawyer's firm, paragraph (b) provides that Rule 1.10 is inapplicable to a representation governed by this rule except as provided by paragraph (a)(2). Paragraph (a)(2) requires the participating lawyer to comply with Rule 1.10 when the lawyer knows that the lawyer's firm is disqualified by Rules 1.7 or 1.9(a). By virtue of paragraph (b), however, a lawyer's participation in a short-term limited legal services program will not preclude the lawyer's firm from undertaking or continuing the representation of a client with interests adverse to a client being represented under the program's auspices. Nor will the personal disqualification of a lawyer participating in the program be imputed to other lawyers participating in the program.

If, after commencing a short-term limited representation in accordance with this rule, a lawyer undertakes to represent the client in the matter on an ongoing basis, Rules 1.7, 1.9(a), and 1.10 become applicable.

Rules 7.1 - 7.5 Information About Legal Services

Rule: 7.1 Communications Concerning a Lawyer's Services

A lawyer may, on the lawyer's own behalf, on behalf of a partner or associate, or on behalf of any other lawyer affiliated with the lawyer or the lawyer's law firm, use or participate in the use of any form of public communication that is not false, fraudulent, misleading, or deceptive. A communication shall not:

(a) contain a material misrepresentation of fact or law, or omit a fact necessary to make the statement considered as a whole not materially misleading;

(b) be likely to create an unjustified expectation about results the lawyer can achieve, or state or imply that the lawyer can achieve results by means that violate the Rules of Professional Conduct or other law; or

(c) compare the lawyer's services with other lawyers' services, unless the comparison can be factually substantiated.

Comment

This rule governs all communications about a lawyer's services, including advertising permitted by Rule 7.2. Whatever means are used to make known a lawyer's services, statements about them should be truthful. The prohibition in paragraph (b) of statements that may create "an unjustified expectation" would ordinarily preclude advertisements about results obtained on behalf of a client, such as the amount of a damage award or the lawyer's record in obtaining favorable verdicts, and would ordinarily preclude advertisements containing client endorsements. Such information may create the unjustified expectation that similar results can be obtained for others without reference to the specific factual and legal circumstances.

Rule: 7.2 Advertising

(a) Subject to the provisions of these rules, a lawyer may advertise.

(b) A copy or recording of an advertisement or communication shall be kept for two years after its last dissemination along with a record of when and where it was used.

(c) A lawyer shall not give anything of value to a person for recommending the lawyer's services, except that a lawyer may:
  (i) pay the reasonable cost of advertising or communication permitted by this rule;
  (ii) participate in, and pay the usual charges of, a not-for-profit lawyer referral service or other legal service organization that satisfies the requirements of Rule 6.3(b); and
  (iii) pay for a law practice in accordance with Rule 1.17.

Comment

To assist the public in obtaining legal services, lawyers should be allowed to make known their services not only through reputation but also through organized information campaigns in the form of advertising. Advertising involves an active quest for clients, contrary to the tradition that a lawyer should not seek clientele. However, the public's need to know about legal services can be fulfilled in part through advertising. This need is particularly acute in the case of persons of moderate means who have not made extensive use of legal services. The interest in expanding public information about legal services ought to prevail over considerations of tradition. Nevertheless, advertising by lawyers entails the risk of practices that are misleading or overreaching.

Neither this rule nor Rule 7.3 prohibits communications authorized by law, such as notice to members of a class in a class action.

RECORD OF ADVERTISING

Paragraph (b) requires that a record of the content and use of advertising be kept in order to facilitate enforcement of these rules.

PAYING OTHERS TO RECOMMEND A LAWYER

A lawyer is allowed to pay for advertising permitted by these rules and for the purchase of a law practice in accordance with the provisions of MRPC 1.17, but otherwise is not permitted to pay another person for channeling professional work. But see MRPC 1.5(e). This restriction does not prevent an organization or person other than the lawyer from advertising or recommending the lawyer's services. Thus, a legal aid agency or prepaid legal services plan may pay to advertise legal services provided under its auspices. Likewise, a lawyer may participate in not-for-profit lawyer referral programs and pay the usual fees charged by such programs. Paragraph (c) does not prohibit paying regular compensation to an assistant, such as a secretary, to prepare communications permitted by these rules.

Rule: 7.3 Direct Contact with Prospective Clients

(a) A lawyer shall not solicit professional employment from a prospective client with whom the lawyer has no family or prior professional relationship when a significant motive for the lawyer's doing so is the lawyer's pecuniary gain. The term "solicit" includes contact in person, by telephone or telegraph, by letter or other writing, or by other communication directed to a specific recipient, but does not include letters addressed or advertising circulars distributed generally to persons not known to need legal services of the kind provided by the lawyer in a particular matter, but who are so situated that they might in general find such services useful, nor does the term "solicit" include "sending truthful and nondeceptive letters to potential clients known to face particular legal problems" as elucidated in Shapero v Kentucky Bar Ass'n, 486 US 466, 468; 108 S Ct 1916; 100 L Ed 2d 475 (1988).

(b) A lawyer shall not solicit professional employment from a prospective client by written or recorded communication or by in-person or telephone contact even when not otherwise prohibited by paragraph (a), if:

    (1) the prospective client has made known to the lawyer a desire not to be solicited by the lawyer; or

    (2) the solicitation involves coercion, duress or harassment.

Comment

There is a potential for abuse inherent in direct contact by a lawyer with a prospective client known to need legal services. These forms of contact between a lawyer and a prospective client subject the layperson to the private importuning of the trained advocate in a direct interpersonal encounter. The prospective client, who may already feel overwhelmed by the circumstances giving rise to the need for legal services, may find it difficult to evaluate fully all available alternatives with reasoned judgment and appropriate self-interest in the face of the lawyer's presence and insistence upon being retained immediately. The situation is fraught with the possibility of undue influence, intimidation, and overreaching.

However, the United States Supreme Court has modified the traditional ban on written solicitation. Shapero v Kentucky Bar Ass'n, 486 US 466; 108 S Ct 1916; 100 L Ed 2d 475 (1988). Paragraph (a) of this rule is therefore modified to the extent required by the Shapero decision.

The potential for abuse inherent in direct solicitation of prospective clients justifies its partial prohibition, particularly since lawyer advertising and the communication permitted under these rules are alternative means of communicating necessary information to those who may be in need of legal services.

Advertising and permissible communication make it possible for a prospective client to be informed about the need for legal services, and about the qualifications of available lawyers and law firms, without subjecting the prospective client to impermissible persuasion that may overwhelm the client's judgment.

The use of general advertising and communications permitted under Shapero to transmit information from lawyer to prospective client, rather than impermissible direct contact, will help to assure that the information flows cleanly as well as freely. Advertising is out in public view, thus subject to scrutiny by those who know the lawyer. The contents of advertisements and communications permitted under Rule 7.2 are permanently recorded so that they cannot be disputed and may be shared with others who know the lawyer. This potential for informal review is itself likely to help guard against statements and claims that might constitute false or misleading communications, in violation of Rule 7.1. The contents of some impermissible direct conversations between a lawyer and a prospective client can be disputed and are not subject to third-party scrutiny. Consequently they are much more likely to approach (and occasionally cross) the dividing line between accurate representations and those that are false and misleading.

There is far less likelihood that a lawyer would engage in abusive practices against an individual with whom the lawyer has a prior family or professional relationship or where the lawyer is motivated by considerations other than the lawyer's pecuniary gain. Consequently, the general prohibition in Rule 7.3(a) is not applicable in those situations.

This rule is not intended to prohibit a lawyer from contacting representatives of organizations or groups that may be interested in establishing a group or prepaid legal plan for its members, insureds, beneficiaries, or other third parties for the purpose of informing such entities of the availability of, and detail concerning, the plan or arrangement that the lawyer or the lawyer's firm is willing to offer. This form of communication is not directed to a specific prospective client known to need legal services related to a particular matter. Rather, it is usually addressed to an individual acting in a fiduciary capacity seeking a supplier of legal services for others who may, if they choose, become prospective clients of the lawyer. Under these circumstances, the activity which the lawyer undertakes in communicating with such representatives and the type of information transmitted to the individual are functionally similar to and serve the same purpose as advertising permitted under these rules.

Rule: 7.4 Communication of Fields of Practice

A lawyer may communicate the fact that the lawyer does or does not practice in particular fields of law.

Comment

This rule permits a lawyer to indicate areas of practice in communications about the lawyer's services, for example, in a telephone directory or other advertising. If a lawyer practices only in certain fields, or will not accept matters except in such fields, the lawyer is permitted to indicate that fact.

Rule: 7.5 Firm Names and Letterheads

(a) A lawyer shall not use a firm name, letterhead or other professional designation that violates Rule 7.1. A trade name may be used by a lawyer in private practice if it does not imply a connection with a government agency or with a public or charitable legal services organization and it is not otherwise in violation of Rule 7.1.

(b) A law firm with offices in more than one jurisdiction may use the same name in each jurisdiction, but identification of the lawyers in an office of the firm shall indicate the jurisdictional limitations on those not licensed to practice in the jurisdiction where the office is located.

(c) The name of a lawyer holding a public office shall not be used in the name of a law firm, or in communications on its behalf, during any substantial period in which the lawyer is not actively and regularly practicing with the firm.

(d) Lawyers may state or imply that they practice in a partnership or other organization only when that is the fact.

Comment

A firm may be designated by the names of all or some of its members, by the names of deceased members where there has been a continuing succession in the firm's identity or by a trade name such as the "ABC Legal Clinic." Although the United States Supreme Court has held that legislation may prohibit the use of trade names in professional practice, use of such names in law practice is acceptable so long as it is not misleading. If a private firm uses a trade name that includes a geographical name such as "Springfield Legal Clinic," an express disclaimer that it is a public legal aid agency may be required to avoid a misleading implication. It may be observed that any firm name including the name of a deceased partner is, strictly speaking, a trade name. The use of such names to designate law firms has proven a useful means of identification. However, it is misleading to use the name of a lawyer not associated with the firm or with a predecessor of the firm.

With regard to paragraph (d), lawyers sharing office facilities, but who are not in fact partners, may not denominate themselves as, for example, "Smith and Jones," for that title suggests partnership in the practice of law.

Rules 8.1 - 8.5 Maintaining the Integrity of the Profession

Rule: 8.1 Bar Admission and Disciplinary Matters

(a) An applicant for admission to the bar, or a lawyer in connection with a bar admission application or in connection with a disciplinary matter, shall not
    (1) knowingly make a false statement of material fact, or
    (2) fail to disclose a fact necessary to correct a misapprehension known by the person to have arisen in the matter, or knowingly fail to respond to a lawful demand for information from an admissions or disciplinary authority, except that this rule does not require disclosure of information protected by Rule 1.6.
(b) An applicant for admission to the bar
    (1) shall not engage in the unauthorized practice of law (this does not apply to activities permitted under MCR 8.120), and
    (2) has a continuing obligation, until the date of admission, to inform the standing committee on character and fitness, in writing, if any answers in the applicant's affidavit of personal history change or cease to be true.

Comment

The duty imposed by this rule extends to persons seeking admission to the bar as well as to lawyers. Hence, if a person makes a material false statement in connection with an application for admission, it may be the basis for subsequent disciplinary action if the person is admitted, and in any event may be relevant in a subsequent admission application. The duty imposed by this rule applies to a lawyer's own admission or discipline as well as that of others. Thus, it is a separate professional offense for a lawyer to knowingly make a misrepresentation or omission in connection with a disciplinary investigation of the lawyer's own conduct. This rule also requires affirmative clarification of any misunderstanding on the part of the admissions or disciplinary authority of which the person involved becomes aware.

This rule is subject to the provisions of the Fifth Amendment of the United States Constitution and to article 1, section 17 of the Michigan Constitution. A person relying on such a provision in response to a question, however, should do so openly and not use the right of nondisclosure as a justification for failure to comply with this rule.

A lawyer representing an applicant for admission to the bar, or representing a lawyer who is the subject of a disciplinary inquiry or proceeding, is governed by the rules applicable to the client-lawyer relationship.

Rule: 8.2 Judicial and Legal Officials

(a) A lawyer shall not make a statement that the lawyer knows to be false or with reckless disregard as to its truth or falsity concerning the qualifications or integrity of a judge, adjudicative officer, or public legal officer, or of a candidate for election or appointment to judicial or legal office.

(b) A lawyer who is a candidate for judicial office shall comply with the applicable provisions of the Code of Judicial Conduct as provided under Canon 5.

Comment

Assessments by lawyers are relied on in evaluating the professional or personal fitness of persons being considered for election or appointment to judicial office and to public legal offices, such as attorney general, prosecuting attorney and public defender. Expressing honest and candid opinions on such matters contributes to improving the administration of justice. Conversely, false statements by a lawyer can unfairly undermine public confidence in the administration of justice.

To maintain the fair and independent administration of justice, lawyers are encouraged to continue traditional efforts to defend judges and courts unjustly criticized.

Rule: 8.3 Reporting Professional Misconduct

(a) A lawyer having knowledge that another lawyer has committed a significant violation of the Rules of Professional Conduct that raises a substantial question as to that lawyer's honesty, trustworthiness, or fitness as a lawyer shall inform the Attorney Grievance Commission.

(b) A lawyer having knowledge that a judge has committed a significant violation of the Code of Judicial Conduct that raises a substantial question as to the judge's honesty, trustworthiness, or fitness for office shall inform the Judicial Tenure Commission.

(c) This rule does not require disclosure of:

    (1) information otherwise protected by Rule 1.6; or

    (2) information gained by a lawyer while serving as an employee or volunteer of the substance abuse counseling program of the State Bar of Michigan, to the extent the information would be protected under

Rule 1.6 from disclosure if it were a communication between lawyer and client.

Comment

Self-regulation of the legal profession requires that members of the profession initiate disciplinary investigation when they know of a violation of the Rules of Professional Conduct. Lawyers have a similar obligation with respect to judicial misconduct. An apparently isolated violation may indicate a pattern of misconduct that only a disciplinary investigation can uncover. Reporting a violation is especially important where the victim is unlikely to discover the offense.

A report about misconduct is not required where it would involve violation of Rule 1.6. However, a lawyer should encourage a client to consent to disclosure where prosecution would not substantially prejudice the client's interests. Because confidentiality is essential to encourage lawyers and judges to seek treatment, information received in the course of providing counseling services in the State Bar's lawyers and judges assistance program is exempt from the reporting requirement to the extent it would be protected under Rule 1.6 if it were a communication between lawyer and client.

If a lawyer were obliged to report every violation of the rules, the failure to report any violation would itself be a professional offense. Such a requirement existed in many jurisdictions but proved to be unenforceable. This rule limits the reporting obligation to those offenses that a self-regulating profession must vigorously endeavor to prevent. A measure of judgment is, therefore, required in complying with the provisions of this rule. The term "substantial" refers to the seriousness of the possible offense and not the quantum of evidence of which the lawyer is aware.

The duty to report professional misconduct does not apply to a lawyer retained to represent a lawyer whose professional conduct is in question. Such a situation is governed by the rules applicable to the client-lawyer relationship.

Rule: 8.4 Misconduct

It is professional misconduct for a lawyer to:
(a) violate or attempt to violate the Rules of Professional Conduct, knowingly assist or induce another to do so, or do so through the acts of another;
(b) engage in conduct involving dishonesty, fraud, deceit, misrepresentation, or violation of the criminal law, where such conduct reflects adversely on the lawyer's honesty, trustworthiness, or fitness as a lawyer;
(c) engage in conduct that is prejudicial to the administration of justice;

(d) state or imply an ability to influence improperly a government agency or official; or

(e) knowingly assist a judge or judicial officer in conduct that is a violation of the Code of Judicial Conduct or other law.

Comment

Many kinds of illegal conduct reflect adversely on fitness to practice law, such as offenses involving fraud and the offense of wilful failure to file an income tax return. However, some kinds of offenses carry no such implication. Traditionally, the distinction was drawn in terms of offenses involving "moral turpitude." That concept can be construed to include offenses concerning some matters of personal morality, such as adultery and comparable offenses, that have no specific connection to fitness for the practice of law. Although a lawyer is personally answerable to the entire criminal law, a lawyer should be professionally answerable only for offenses that indicate lack of those characteristics relevant to law practice. Offenses involving violence, dishonesty, breach of trust, or serious interference with the administration of justice are in that category. A pattern of repeated offenses, even ones of minor significance when considered separately, can indicate indifference to legal obligation.

A lawyer may refuse to comply with an obligation imposed by law upon a good-faith belief that no valid obligation exists. The provisions of Rule 1.2(c) concerning a good-faith challenge to the validity, scope, meaning, or application of the law apply to challenges of legal regulation of the practice of law. See also Rule 3.4(c).

Lawyers holding public office assume legal responsibilities going beyond those of other citizens. A lawyer's abuse of public office can suggest an inability to fulfill the professional role of attorney. The same is true of abuse of positions of private trust such as trustee, executor, administrator, guardian, agent, and such as officer, director, or manager of a corporation or other organization.

Rule: 8.5 Disciplinary Authority; Choice of Law

(a) Disciplinary Authority. A lawyer admitted to practice in this jurisdiction is subject to the disciplinary authority of this jurisdiction, regardless where the lawyer's conduct occurs. A lawyer not admitted in this jurisdiction is also subject to the disciplinary authority of this jurisdiction if the lawyer provides or offers to provide any legal services in this jurisdiction. A lawyer may be subject to the disciplinary authority of both this jurisdiction and another jurisdiction for the same conduct.

(b) **Choice of Law.** In any exercise of the disciplinary authority of this jurisdiction, the rules of professional conduct to be applied shall be as follows:

    (1)   for conduct in connection with a matter pending before a tribunal, the rules of the jurisdiction in which the tribunal sits, unless the rules of the tribunal provide otherwise; and

    (2)   for any other conduct, the rules of the jurisdiction in which the conduct occurred, or, if the predominant effect of the conduct is in a different jurisdiction, the rules of that jurisdiction shall be applied to the conduct; a lawyer shall not be subject to discipline if the lawyer's conduct conforms to the rules of a jurisdiction in which the lawyer reasonably believes the predominant effect of the lawyer's conduct will occur.

Comment

DISCIPLINARY AUTHORITY

It is longstanding law that the conduct of a lawyer admitted to practice in this jurisdiction is subject to the disciplinary authority of this jurisdiction. Extension of the disciplinary authority of this jurisdiction to other lawyers who provide or offer to provide legal services in this jurisdiction is for the protection of the citizens of this jurisdiction. Reciprocal enforcement of a jurisdiction's disciplinary findings and sanctions will further advance the purposes of this rule. The fact that a lawyer is subject to the disciplinary authority of this jurisdiction may be a factor in determining whether personal jurisdiction may be asserted over the lawyer in civil matters.

CHOICE OF LAW

A lawyer potentially may be subject to more than one set of rules of professional conduct that impose different obligations. The lawyer may be licensed to practice in more than one jurisdiction with differing rules, or may be admitted to practice before a particular court with rules that differ from those of the jurisdiction or jurisdictions in which the lawyer is licensed to practice. Additionally, the lawyer's conduct may involve significant contacts with more than one jurisdiction.

Paragraph (b) seeks to resolve such potential conflicts. Its premise is that minimizing conflicts between rules, as well as uncertainty about which rules are applicable, is in the best interests of clients, the profession, and those who are authorized to regulate the profession. Accordingly, paragraph (b) provides that any particular conduct of a lawyer shall be subject to only one set of rules of professional conduct; makes the determination of which set of rules applies to particular conduct as straightforward as possible, consistent with recognition of appropriate regulatory interests of relevant jurisdictions; and protects from discipline those lawyers who act reasonably in the face of uncertainty.

Paragraph (b)(1) provides, as to a lawyer's conduct relating to a proceeding pending before a tribunal, that the lawyer shall be subject only to the rules of the jurisdiction in which the tribunal sits unless the rules of the tribunal, including its choice of law rule, provide otherwise. As to all other conduct, including conduct in anticipation of a proceeding not yet pending before a tribunal, paragraph (b)(2) provides that a lawyer shall be subject to the rules of the jurisdiction in which the lawyer's conduct occurred or, if the predominant effect of the conduct is in another jurisdiction, the lawyer shall be subject to the rules of that jurisdiction. In the case of conduct in anticipation of a proceeding that is likely to be before a tribunal, the predominant effect of such conduct could be either where the conduct occurred, where the tribunal sits, or in another jurisdiction.

When a lawyer's conduct involves significant contacts with more than one jurisdiction, it may not be clear initially whether the predominant effect of the lawyer's conduct will occur in a jurisdiction other than the one in which the conduct actually did occur. So long as the lawyer's conduct conforms to the rules of a jurisdiction in which the lawyer reasonably believes the predominant effect will occur, the lawyer shall not be subject to discipline under this rule.

If two admitting jurisdictions were to proceed against a lawyer for the same conduct, they should, applying this rule, identify the same governing ethics rules. They should take all appropriate steps to see that they do apply the same rule to the same conduct and should avoid proceeding against a lawyer on the basis of inconsistent rules.

The choice of law provision applies to lawyers engaged in transnational practice, unless international law, treaties, or other agreements between regulatory authorities in the affected jurisdictions provide otherwise.

www.ingramcontent.com/pod-product-compliance
Lightning Source LLC
Chambersburg PA
CBHW060620200326
41521CB00007B/826